THE
SAMSUNG®
Galaxy S8

COMPLETE
UNOFFICIAL GUIDE

BP BinaryPublisher.com

The Samsung Galaxy S8 Complete Unofficial Guide

The Samsung Galaxy S8 Complete Unofficial Guide

Binary Publisher, LLC

Binary Publisher, LLC

Pittsburgh, PA

Contents

Introduction

The Samsung Galaxy S8 - Complete Unofficial Guide explains all of the powerful features of the Galaxy S8 in an easy to follow format and shows you exactly how to use them.

Congratulations to you for becoming the owner of one of the most advanced pieces of technology that exist - The Samsung Galaxy S8. Unfortunately, many owners of the S8 will never actually use the majority of its capabilities. The Samsung Galaxy S8 - Complete Unofficial Guide aims to change that by providing you easy to follow, step by step instructions designed to help you master the Galaxy S8's most important features quickly.

If you have used a previous generation of the Galaxy such as the infamous S7, S6, S5 or other models, then this guide will show you exactly what has changed. If, on the other hand, you have never used a Galaxy device before, this guide will help you to determine if the Galaxy S8 is the right model of smart phone for you.

Previous use of a Samsung smart phone device is helpful but certainly not required.

This book was written to make you familiar with the different features and functions of the Samsung Galaxy S8, S*+ and the S8 Edge.

As you probably already know, many in this world strive want to have the best phone. Many desire to have the latest model of the smartphone be it a Samsung, Apple or another brand of phone. Sometimes people purchase high-end phones with no knowledge of how to use them.

One goal of The Samsung Galaxy S8 - Complete Unofficial Guide is to allow everyone use a cell phone with the same efficacy as the rest. This book makes it easier for you to understand your smartphone as it has all your questions and queries answered at one place. This book has touches the most used features and important topics for the Samsung Galaxy S8.

The Samsung Galaxy S8 - Complete Unofficial Guide describes nearly every option, every feature and every function that will be available on your phone, while using large screen shots and easy to follow step-by-step instructions.

1

What's New

Samsung has released two new S8 models – the S8 "base" and another referred to as the S8 Plus. The S8 Plus has a slightly better display in terms of size along with a battery yielding slightly more capacity to power it. We have outlined the majority of the new features of the Samsung Galaxy S8 and S8 Plus below along with a chart for comparison of the various technical specifications.

- **Design -** The most noticeable change to the Galaxy S8 is the size of it's screen. The base S8 model boasts a 5.8 inch screen while the S8 Plus comes in at over a full inch larger than it's predecessor at 6.2 inches. The display resolution is more or less unchanged from the S7 models. Also notable is the absence of the large physical home button that has now been replaced by a software version.
- **Dex Dock -** This $150 add-on device allows you to easily turn your Galaxy S8 into a desktop PC by connecting it to a monitor, keyboard and mouse through the USB-C port. Although this configuration won't win any performance awards, it is reportedly very straightforward and easy to use by beta testers. Dex Dock has not been completely implemented at the time of this publication. Samsung is still rolling out features although the actual Dex Dock hardware can be purchased for around $150.
- **Facial/Iris Scanner -** New to the S8 is the facial/iris scanner which is used in conjunction with Samsung's new facial recognition feature for improved phone security.
- **Force Touch -** The S8's home button is now integrated into the screen through the use of a hapatic feedback sensor which senses the amount of pressure applied to the lower half of the screen.
- **Performance -** The processor has gone from quad core to eight core, each of which are slightly faster than those found in the S7 which makes for an overall smoother user experience. In addition, the S8 comes packaged with the Android 7.0 Nougat operating system, which also helps to improve overall performance over its predecessor Android Marshmallow.
- **Camera -** The front facing (selfie) camera has been improved over the S7 from 5 megapixels to 8. All other camera features including the rear facing camera and video capturing capability remain the same. In summary, the selfie camera has been improved, while the standard camera remains unchanged.
- **Ports -** Here the focus is on what hasn't changed rather than what has, due to the decision to retain the 3.5mm headphone jack which another notable phone manufacturer has opted to remove from their latest models. USB-C is now utilized instead of the Micro USB for data transfer and charging.
- **Bixby -** Bixby consists of three parts – Voice, Vision and Home. Bixby Voice is Samsung's virtual assistant and voice recognition software that launched in 2017 which aims to compete with Apple's Siri, Microsoft's Cortana and Amazon's Alexa. Bixby is only available on the S8 models at the time of this publication and although Bixby Voice holds a lot of promise, some critics complain that it doesn't perform as well as it's competitors. Not all Samsung Galaxy S8 devices are being shipped with Bixby pre-installed due to the fact that Samsung is still rolling out many core features of Bixby at the time of this publication.

Galaxy S8 vs S7 Comparison

	Galaxy S8	Galaxy S8 Plus	Galaxy S7	Galaxy S7 Edge
Display size, resolution	5.8-inch; 2,960 x 1,440 pixels	6.2-inch; 2,960 x 1,440 pixels	5.1-inch; 2,560 x 1,440 pixels	5.5-inch; 2,560 x 1,440 pixels
Pixel density	570ppi	529ppi	576ppi	534ppi
Dimensions (inches)	5.86 x 2.68 x 0.32 in.	6.3 x 2.9 x 0.32 in.	5.6 x 2.7 x 0.3 in.	5.9 x 2.9 x 0.3 in.
Dimensions (millimeters)	148.9 x 68.1 x 8 mm	159.5 x 73.4 x 8.1 mm	142.4 x 69.6 x 7.9 mm	150.9 x 72.6 x 7.7 mm
Weight (ounces, grams)	5.5 oz.; 155g	6.1 oz.; 173g	5.4 oz.; 152g	5.5 oz.; 157g
Mobile software	Android 7.0 Nougat	Android 7.0 Nougat	Android 6.0 Marshmallow	Android 6.0 Marshmallow
Camera (megapixels)	12	12	12	12
Front-facing camera (megapixels)	8	8	5	5
Video capture	4K	4K	4K	4K
Processor	2.35GHz + 1.9GHz eight- core Qualcomm Snapdragon 835 or Samsung eight-core Exynos 8895 (2.35GHz + 1.7GHz)	2.35GHz + 1.9GHz eight- core Qualcomm Snapdragon 835 or Samsung eight-core Exynos 8895 (2.35GHz + 1.7GHz)	2.15GHz + 1.6GHz quad- core Qualcomm Snapdragon 820	2.15GHz + 1.6GHz quad- core Qualcomm Snapdragon 820
Storage	64GB	64GB	32GB, 64GB (varies by region)	32GB, 64GB (varies by region)
RAM	4GB	4GB	4GB	4GB
Expandable storage	2TB	2TB	200GB	200GB
Battery (all nonremovable)	3,000mAh	3,500mAh	3,000mAh	3,600mAh
Fingerprint sensor	Back cover	Back cover	Home button	Home button
Data/Power Connector	USB-C	USB-C	Micro-USB	Micro-USB
Special features	Water-resistant; wireless charging; Gigabit LTE-ready	Water-resistant, wireless charging, Gigabit LTE-ready	Water-resistant, wireless charging	Water-resistant, wireless charging
Price off-contract (USD) at launch	AT&T: $750; Verizon: $720; T-Mobile: $750; Sprint: $750; U.S. Cellular: TBA	AT&T: $850; Verizon: $840; T-Mobile: $850; Sprint: $850; U.S. Cellular: TBA	AT&T: $695; Verizon: $672; T-Mobile: $670; Sprint: $650; US Cellular: $672	AT&T: $795; Verizon: $792; T-Mobile: $780; Sprint: $750; U.S. Cellular: $780

2

Preparing the Galaxy S8 or Galaxy S8+ for First Use

Now that you've gotten your Galaxy S8 or Galaxy S8+, you'll likely want to get up and running with it as quickly as possible.

Note: From here on, this book uses the term "Galaxy S8" to refer to both the Galaxy S8 and the Galaxy S8+ together when they work the same way. For those few points where the Galaxy S8 and the Galaxy S8+ differ, the book specifies which model it's talking about.

This chapter covers the main considerations for setting up your Galaxy S8:

- Inserting a SIM card and micro SD card
- Giving the phone an initial charge (if necessary)
- Making the right decisions in the setup routine
- Transferring data from your existing Android device (also if necessary)

At the end of the chapter, we'll also take a quick look at charging the S8 before moving on to navigating the user interface in the next chapter.

Add Your SIM Card and Micro SD Card

Some carriers and stores provide the Galaxy S8 with a SIM card already inserted in it. If so, you're good to go—except that you'll likely want to add a micro SD card to boost the phone's storage. Few carriers provide a micro SD card for you, but some stores will insert a micro SD card if you pay for it.

The Galaxy S8 has an micro SD card slot in the same tray as the SIM card. You can use either a micro SDHC card or a micro SDXC card in the micro SD slot. We'll look at what those terms mean in just a moment.

Dual-SIM Galaxy S8 Models: Two SIMs, or SIM + SD

Most Galaxy S8 models are single-SIM models, as described in the main text. But in some markets Samsung also sells dual-SIM models of Galaxy S8. If you have a dual-SIM Galaxy S8, you can choose between inserting two SIM cards and inserting a single SIM card and one micro SD card.

Add a SIM Card

The Galaxy S8 takes a nano-SIM. This is currently the smallest size of SIM card in widespread use. If your phone came without a SIM, order one from your carrier (if you have an existing plan you will use) or online from the carrier you will use.

Follow these steps to insert a SIM card:

1. When you've got the SIM card, push the included SIM removal tool or the straightened end of a paperclip into the hole next to the SIM slot at the top of the Galaxy S8.
2. Use your fingernails to pull out the SIM tray.

Caution: Look carefully to make sure the hole you're planning to insert the SIM removal tool in is the SIM ejection hole. The microphone hole on the top of the Galaxy S8 looks similar but will not appreciate being prodded with a sharp object.

3. Once you've removed the SIM tray, insert the SIM card in it. The SIM card fits in only one way, so there shouldn't be any confusion.
4. Before reinserting the SIM tray, insert the micro SD if you're going to use one. See the next section for details.

5. Once Android is running, the Galaxy S8 warns you if it detects that the SIM tray is not pushed in

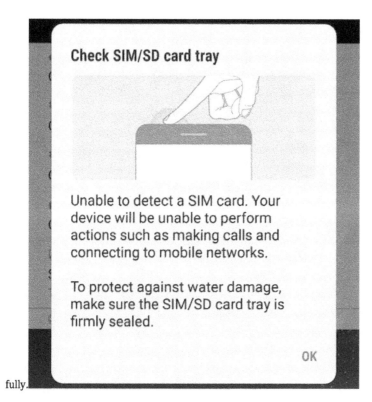

Check SIM/SD card tray

Unable to detect a SIM card. Your device will be unable to perform actions such as making calls and connecting to mobile networks.

To protect against water damage, make sure the SIM/SD card tray is firmly sealed.

OK

fully.

Add a Micro SD Card

Most Galaxy S8 and Galaxy S8+ models come with 64GB of built-in storage. This is plenty to get you started, but you'll probably want to add storage to give yourself more space. 64GB doesn't go all that far if you store photos (large files), music (larger files), and videos (which can be huge) on your phone.

Because the micro SD card slot is in the SIM card tray (or vice-versa, if you prefer), swapping micro SD cards is more of a pain on the Galaxy S8 than it is on any device with a standalone micro SD card slot. Normally, it's best to power off the phone before you remove the SIM tray, because if you don't, you may need to restart your phone to get the SIM working again.

So whereas with another device you might get several micro SD cards, put different content on them, and switch them in and out as needed, with the Galaxy S8 you're better off getting a single micro SD card and keeping it in place. Normally, that'll mean getting either a 256GB SD card—the highest-capacity micro SD card the Galaxy S8 accepts—or the highest-capacity card you can afford.

Like the SIM card, the micro SD card fits in the tray only one way.

Charge the Galaxy S8

If you're lucky, the battery in your Galaxy S8 will contain enough power for you to start setup as soon as you take the phone out of its box. If not, you may need to plug it in to charge. Use the charger and cable that came with the phone, because they're designed to charge the battery quickly and safely.

3

Configuring the Galaxy S8 For First Use

The device can be used once it has been charged at the SIM card is loaded. Press and hold the **Power** button for a few seconds to start the phone. The first time you start your Galaxy S8, the phone automatically walks you through an easy-to-follow setup routine. The following sections in this chapter walk you through the major decisions on the screens in the setup routine and cover the main decisions and actions you need to take when setting up your Galaxy S8.

A.Welcome Screen: Choose Your Language

Before you begin this setup process, make sure that you have at least 10 minutes to devote to its completion because it contains many steps. Begin setting up your phone for first use by selecting the language you wish to use.

a. Scroll through the *language list* in the middle of the screen to select the language you want the phone to use, and then tap the **Start**  ⿻ ⿻ .₁₁ 49%🔋

button.The one thing worth noting here is that you can tap the **Accessibility** button to start using accessibility options during setup. For example, if you have difficulty seeing the screen, you can choose a larger font size. Or you can turn on the *Voice Assistant* feature, which announces the names of on-screen items.

2. Wi-Fi Screen: Join a Wi-Fi Network

a. On the Wi-Fi screen, tap the appropriate wireless network in the list. Type the network's password in the dialog box that opens, and then tap the **Connect** button.

Welcome!

Wi-Fi

ADVANCED

ON   ⊠ ENGLISH (UNITED STATES) ▼

Apex2

OutOfGrange

SCHOOL_AP_05

SCHOOL_VISITOR_NETWORK

                                          START ›
InGrange

SKY2ED34

+   Add network

                                ,   ☆
                              CY CALL   ACCESSIBILITY

‹   NEXT ›

If the network you want doesn't appear, follow these steps to add it:

1. Tap the **Add Network** button at the bottom of the list of networks to display the *Add Network* dialog box.
2. Type the network's name in the *Network Name* box.
3. Tap the *Security* pop-up menu and then tap the security type, such as WPA/WPA2/FT PSK.
4. Type the *password*

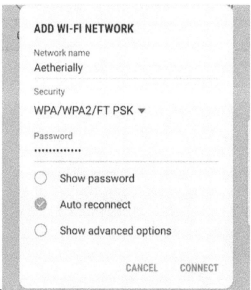

ADD WI-FI NETWORK

Network name
Aetherially

Security
WPA/WPA2/FT PSK ▼

Password
•••••••••••

○ Show password

◉ Auto reconnect

○ Show advanced options

CANCEL   CONNECT

5. Tap the **Connect** button.

b. When your phone is connected to a Wi-Fi network, tap the **Next** button. The *Terms and Conditions* screen appears.

3. Terms and Conditions screen: Accept the Terms and Conditions

To complete the setup process up and use your Galaxy S8, you must accept the End User License Agreement and the Privacy Policy. You can choose whether or not to consent to provide diagnostic data and whether or not to receive marketing information.

?. Select the radio buttons next to *End User License Agreement* and *Privacy Policy* at minimum to continue. These options are mandatory and the other are optional. Click the *Learn more* links to read what you are agreeing to.

Terms and conditions

○ **Agree to all**

○ **End User License Agreement**
Read the End User License Agreement carefully.
It contains important information.
Learn more

○ **Privacy Policy**
User data processed by Samsung is governed
by the Samsung Privacy Policy.
Learn more

○ **Diagnostic data**
Consent to provide diagnostic and usage data
Learn more

○ **Marketing information**
Receive marketing information
Learn more

<   NEXT >

Note: If you're in a hurry to start using your Galaxy S8, you may be tempted to select the *Agree to All* check circle, which checks the other four check circles for you. But usually it's a better idea to check only the *End User License Agreement* check circle and the *Privacy Policy* check circle; check the *Diagnostic Data* check circle as well if you want to provide diagnostic and usage data anonymously to Samsung. You can tap any of the four *Learn More* links on the *Terms and Conditions* screen to find out more about the End User License Agreement, the Privacy Policy, the collection of diagnostic data, and the marketing information that Samsung sends to those who agree to receive it.

Note: Samsung benefits if you provide diagnostic and usage data. You benefit at best only indirectly, in that Samsung may improve its hardware and software as a result of the information it gathers from users, and some of these improvements may eventually be helpful to you.

b. When you tap the **Next** button on the *Terms and Conditions* screen, the *Add Your Account* screen appears.

4. Decide Whether to Add a Google Account (and If So, Which Account)

On the *Add Your Account* screen, you can choose whether to add a Google account to the Galaxy S8. Android is designed to depend so heavily on a Google account that you will normally want to add an

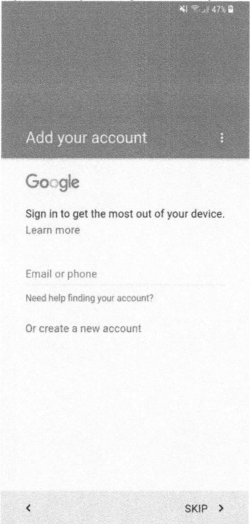

account to your phone.

Note: If you don't yet have a Google account, or if you want to set up a new account for use on this phone, tap the Or *Create a New Account* link on the *Add Your Account* screen. Follow the prompts to create the account.

To add your existing Google account, follow these steps:

    a. Tap the *Email* or *Phone* field. Your phone automatically displays the keyboard.

    b. Type the address for your Google account, or type your phone number.

    c. Tap the **Next** button. (The **Next** button replaces the **Skip** button when you type your email address.) The *Password* screen appears.

    d. Type your password. If you've forgotten it, you can tap the *Forgot Password?* link and follow the instructions to get a new password.

    e. Tap the **Next** button. A screen appears saying that by signing in, you agree to the Terms of Service and the Privacy Policy. You can tap the *Terms of Service* link or the *Privacy Policy* link to see more information about what you're agreeing to.

    f. Tap the **Accept** button if you want to proceed. The *Google Services* screen then appears.

5. Google Services Screen: Choose Which Google Services to Use

If you've added a Google account, use the controls on the Google Services screen to specify which services to use. This is a long screen, so you need to scroll down to reach some of the options.

Google services

You can turn these services on or off at any time for john.random.luser@gmail.com. Data will be used according to Google's Privacy Policy.

If you want to learn more, you can tap each service.

Automatically back up device data (such as Wi-Fi passwords and call history) and app data (such as settings and files stored by apps) to Google Drive.

Use Google's location service to help apps determine your location. Anonymous location data will be sent to Google when your device is on.

Improve location accuracy by allowing apps and services to scan for Wi-Fi and Bluetooth, even when these settings are off.

Help improve your Android experience by automatically sending diagnostic and device and app usage data to Google. This won't be used to identify you and will help improve battery life, app stability, network connectivity, and more.

<   NEXT >

The following list explains the options on the *Google Services* screen. The options have long names, of which the list uses shortened versions.

- **Automatically Back Up Device Data**. Set this switch to On to have your Galaxy S8 automatically back up your data to your Google account. This is normally a good idea. After a software failure, you can restore the data to your phone. Or if you lose your phone, you can restore your data either to a new device (either a phone or a tablet).
- **Use Google's Location Service to Help Apps Determine Your Location.** Set this switch to On if you want to allow apps to use your location data. This feature is good if you want to be able to get information based on where you are, such as hotels or places to eat. If you're more concerned about your privacy, uncheck this box.

- **Improve Location Accuracy.** This switch requires a trickier decision. Android can automatically scan for Wi-Fi networks even when you've turned Wi-Fi off. Android does this scanning in order to improve the accuracy of location services and to detect wireless networks that it may want to add to its database. Set this switch to On if you're happy for this scanning to occur. Set this switch to Off if you need to ration battery power or if you want to implement an "off means off" policy.
- **Help Improve Your Android Experience.** Set this switch to Off if you don't want to send diagnostic data and usage data to Google to help improve its services. You can tap the Help Improve Your Android Experience button to display a dialog box that explains what Google does with the data it gets.

Tip: Be sure to read the paragraph at the bottom of the *Google Services* screen that explains you're agreeing to have your phone automatically download and install updates from Google, your carrier, and your phone's manufacturer, and that these updates may be downloaded across the cellular connection. You can't turn off this settings—all you can do is decide not to proceed with setting up your Google account.

    a. Tap the **Next** button when you've made your choices on the *Google Services* screen.

6. Which Device? Screen: Choose Which Data to Restore, If Any

If your Google account contains backed-up data that you can restore to this phone, the *Which Device?* screen appears as shown:

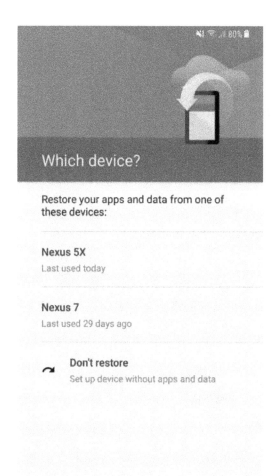

Restore your apps and data from one of these devices:

Nexus 5X
Last used today

Nexus 7
Last used 29 days ago

Don't restore
Set up device without apps and data

If you've got an Android device that has your accounts, apps, and data on it, you can copy these items across to your Galaxy S8. This is usually an easy way of getting your new phone set up with your accounts, apps, and data—but see the nearby sidebar called "Understand the Two Methods of Transferring Data During Setup" before you go ahead.

Understanding the Two Methods of Transferring Data During Setup

The setup routine for the Galaxy S8 includes not one but two methods of transferring data from your old device. The first method, which you access from the Which Device? screen, actually gets data from your

Google account rather than directly from the phone or tablet. The second method is called Smart Switch, and you access it from the Copy Content from Old Device screen, later in the setup process.

- **Which Device?** The *Which Device?* feature is built into Android and transfers the details of your Google account, the apps that you have bought or gotten from the Play Store, and the data backups you have stored online. After you identify the device whose backup you want to use, your new device downloads the data from your Google account and the apps from the Play Store. If you have a Google account set up on your existing device, you'll likely want to use this way to transfer your data to your new phone and install your apps on it.
- **Smart Switch.** *Smart Switch* is a Samsung app and requires the USB Connector hardware device that's included with the Galaxy S8. Smart Switch uses a USB cable to transfer data. It enables you to transfer your photos, your contacts, and your messages from your old device to your new device. Contacts and messages typically contain only a small amount of data, but photos can add up to many gigabytes, so the fast data-transfer speeds of the USB cable are helpful.

To transfer your Google account data, follow these steps from the Which Device? screen:

    a. Tap the button for the device from which you want to copy the data. The *Restore Apps From* screen appears.

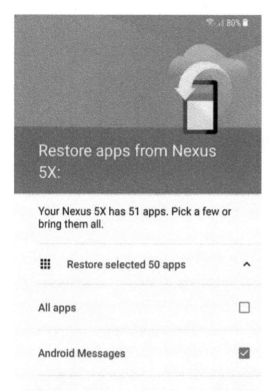

Restore apps from Nexus 5X:

Your Nexus 5X has 51 apps. Pick a few or bring them all.

Restore selected 50 apps

All apps

Android Messages

Calculator

Camera Nexus 7 (official)

Clock

‹   RESTORE ›

b. Tap the *Restore Selected Apps* button to display the list of apps.

Protect your phone

Prevent others from using this phone without your permission by activating device protection features.

Learn more

◉ Set up Face Recognition

○ Set up Fingerprint Scanner

○ Set up Iris Scanner

○ Set up PIN, pattern or password

○ No, thank you

‹   NEXT ›

c. Uncheck the check box for any app you don't want to install on your Galaxy S8.

d. Tap the **Restore** button. The *Protect Your Phone* screen appears.

e. If you haven't been using an Android device, tap the **Don't Restore** button on the *Which Device?* screen instead, and then tap the> button.

Note: Android automatically transfers all the apps you've installed on the other device. But normally it's a good idea to look through the list and remove any apps that you no longer find useful.

7. Protect Your Phone Screen: Set Up Your Unlock Method

Your phone is a treasure trove of sensitive information, so it's vital you protect it against intrusion. From the *Protect Your Phone* screen, you can choose among five means of unlocking your phone:

- **Set Up Face Recognition.** You can set your face to unlock your phone. This is a fun feature but is not practical for everybody and is not considered secure. To unlock the phone with your face, you normally need to raise the phone in front of your face (rather than, say, moving your face over the screen). If you wear spectacles, you may need to remove them. You must set a backup means of unlocking—a PIN, pattern, or password—for times when face recognition fails.

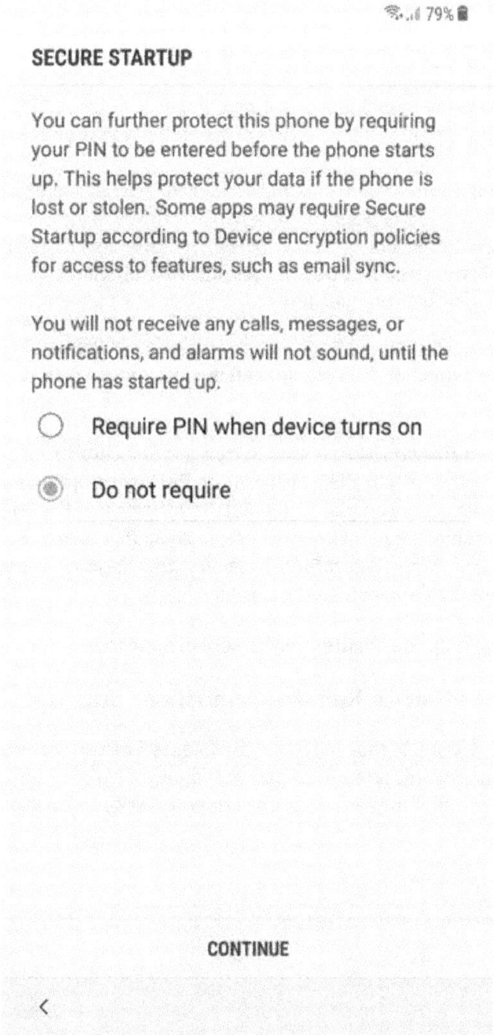
79%
SECURE STARTUP
You can further protect this phone by requiring your PIN to be entered before the phone starts up. This helps protect your data if the phone is lost or stolen. Some apps may require Secure Startup according to Device encryption policies for access to features, such as email sync.
You will not receive any calls, messages, or notifications, and alarms will not sound, until the phone has started up.
Require PIN when device turns on
Do not require
CONTINUE

- **Set Up Fingerprint Scanner.** You can set one or more fingerprints to unlock your phone. This is usually the most convenient means of unlocking. You must set a backup means of unlocking—a PIN, pattern, or password—for when your fingerprint doesn't work.
- **Set Up Iris Scanner.** You can set your Galaxy S8 to scan your iris to unlock the device. This is a quick and convenient way to unlock the phone, but it is not considered as secure as using a fingerprint. If you choose to use iris scanning, you must also set a PIN, pattern, or password as a backup method of unlocking.

Note: After a restart, or after you haven't used your Galaxy S8 for 24 hours or more, you must use your alternative unlock method instead of face, fingerprint, or iris. You can disable this security feature, but it is best to keep it enabled.

- **Set Up PIN, Pattern, or Password.** You can protect your Galaxy S8 with a PIN, a pattern, or a password:
  - **PIN.** You can set a four-digit or longer personal identification number, or PIN. A PIN is an adequate means of security, but you should set a minimum of six digits, and preferably much longer.
  - **Pattern.** You can draw a pattern on a grid of nine dots to unlock your phone. A pattern is not generally considered an adequate form of security for a phone.
  - **Password.** You can set a four-character or longer password. For security, use at least eight characters, preferably more. This is the strongest way of securing your phone.
  - **No, Thank You.** You can refuse to use security measures.

Caution: Never use the *No, Thank You* option on the *Protect Your Phone* screen for your personal phone. The only time to use this setting is for a demonstration phone, and in most cases, even such a phone would be better locked.

To set your unlock method, tap the **Set Up Face Recognition** option button, the **Set Up Fingerprint** option button, the **Set Up Iris** option button, or the **Set Up PIN, Pattern, or Password** option button; tap the **Next** button, and then follow the prompts. For example, on the *Set Up Fingerprint Security* screen, tap the button for the backup means of unlocking that you will use, such as **Password**. Follow the prompts to create the password, and then scan your fingerprint by placing your fingertip repeatedly on the **Home** button and following the feedback that appears on the screen.

When you finish setting up your means of unlocking, the *Secure Startup* screen appears.

8. Secure Startup Screen: Choose Whether to Require Security at Startup

a. On the *Secure Startup* screen, you can choose whether to enable the Secure Startup feature. This feature requires you to enter your PIN, password, or security pattern when your phone turns on. Secure Startup adds another layer of protection for your data, so turning on Secure Startup is

SECURE STARTUP

You can further protect this phone by requiring
your PIN to be entered before the phone starts
up. This helps protect your data if the phone is
lost or stolen. Some apps may require Secure
Startup according to Device encryption policies
for access to features, such as email sync.

You will not receive any calls, messages, or
notifications, and alarms will not sound, until the
phone has started up.

○　Require PIN when device turns on

◉　Do not require

CONTINUE

‹

usually a good idea.

b. If you want to turn on *Secure Startup*, select the ***Require PIN When Device Turns On*** option
button, the***Require Password When Device Turns On*** option button, or the***Require Pattern
When Device Turns On*** option button, depending on your choice of unlock method.

c. If you prefer not to use *Secure Startup*, select the ***Do Not Require*** option button.

d. Either way, tap the ***Continue*** button to proceed with setup.

9. Notifications Screen: Choose Whether to Display Notifications on the Lock Screen

On the *Notifications* screen, you can choose whether notifications appear on the lock screen and, if they

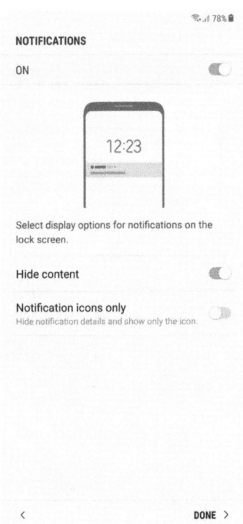

<

DONE >

do, whether their content appears. These are the controls you can set:

- **Notifications switch.** Set the switch at the top of the *Notifications* screen to *On* if you want to have the lock screen display notifications. Otherwise, set this switch to *Off* and skip the rest of this section.
- **Hide Content.** Set this switch to *On* if you want the lock screen to display notifications but not their content. You can then use a notification's type to determine whether you need to unlock your phone and view the notification's content.
- **Notification Icons Only.** Set this switch to *On* if you want to see only the icons of the apps that have raised notifications, not any details about the time or any people involved.

a. After making your choice, tap the **Done** button. The *Samsung Account* screen then appears.

10. Samsung Account Screen: Choose Whether to Add a Samsung Account

The *Samsung Account* screen enables you to add your Samsung account to your Galaxy S8. If you already have a Samsung account, you'll likely want to add it.

Perform this step to add your Samsung account:

a. Tap the **Sign In** button and follow the prompts. If you don't already have a Samsung account, you can tap the **Create Account** button to start the process of creating one. But before you do, scroll down the screen to display information about the benefits of a Samsung account and decide whether you want to create one at this point. If not, tap the **Skip** button, which you'll find at the very bottom of the screen.

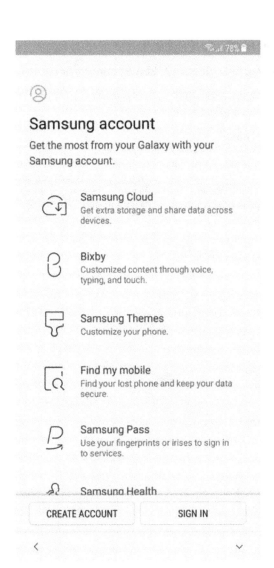

Samsung account

Get the most from your Galaxy with your
Samsung account.

Samsung Cloud
Get extra storage and share data across
devices.

Bixby
Customized content through voice,
typing, and touch.

Samsung Themes
Customize your phone.

Find my mobile
Find your lost phone and keep your data
secure.

Samsung Pass
Use your fingerprints or irises to sign in
to services.

Samsung Health

| CREATE ACCOUNT | SIGN IN |

Note: You don't have to have a Samsung account to set up and use your Galaxy S8, but you do need a
Samsung account to use all its features to the max. Samsung has followed Google's lead in trying to
make a Samsung account indispensable, and it has made considerable progress. Features such as the
Bixby personal assistant; Find My Mobile (which helps you locate your device when it goes missing, and
wipe its contents remotely if necessary; tracking your progress in the Samsung Health app, and sharing
it with others; and getting apps from Samsung's Galaxy Apps store—these features are available only
when you sign in to a Samsung account.

11. Get Your Content Screen: Copy Your Content Across

After you set up your Samsung account or choose to skip adding one, the *Get Your Content* screen appears. This screen enables you to transfer data from your Samsung account (if you've added one), or from another Android device, to your Galaxy S8. For example, if you have photos or contact data on your old phone, you can quickly transfer them to your Galaxy S8. The *Get your content screen* is shown

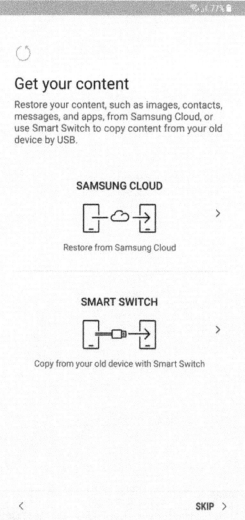

below:

Note: If you don't want to transfer content now, tap the **Skip** button. You can run the *Smart Switch* app at any time to transfer content.

a. To transfer content, tap the **Samsung Cloud** button or the **Smart Switch** button, as appropriate, and then follow the prompts.
b. If you choose to transfer data via Samsung Cloud, select the appropriate phone or tablet in the *Backup Device* pop-up menu on the *Restore Data* screen; select the check circle for each data category you want to restore; and then tap the **Restore** button.

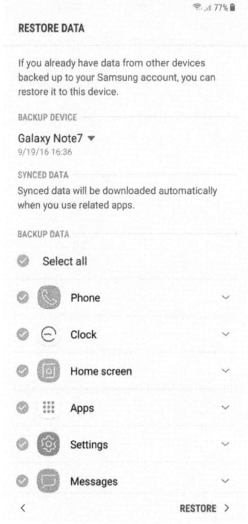

c. If you choose to transfer data via Smart Switch, connect the devices as shown in the illustrations using a USB cable and the Samsung USB adapters included with your phone. After the devices identify each other, select the content you want to transfer, and then tap the **Transfer** button.

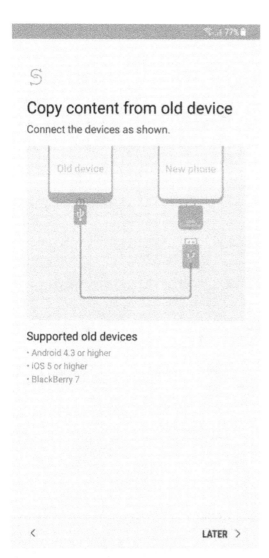

12. More Useful Features Screen

On the *More Useful Features* screen, you can configure the following settings:

- **Secure Your Stuff.** Look to see if the readout on this button shows *On*; this is normally the default setting. If not, you can tap this button to set up the Secure Folder feature.

More useful features

Take a look and see if you want to make any changes.

Secure your stuff

Protect your private data and apps from phishing and other attacks by saving them in a Secure Folder.
ON

Set screen layout

To view more content or content more clearly, set the level of screen zoom, and to view smaller or larger text, set the font size.
Small, Medium

Get weather forecasts

View the weather forecast for your current location on the home screen and in other apps.

○ **Agree to all**

○ Consent to the use of your location by the content provider
Learn more

◉ Consent to turn on Location and change Locating method
Learn more

◉ Receive notifications about changes to the weather.

<   **FINISH** >

- **Set Screen Layout.** Tap this button if you want to change the screen zoom or the font size. In the bottom section of the *More Useful Features* screen, check the appropriate check circles.
- **Agree to All.** Check this check circle to select the three lower check circles in one move. Do this only if you consent to content providers learning your location.
- **Consent to the Use of Your Location by the Content Provider.** Check this check circle if you agree to provide your location in exchange for receiving location-specific information (such as search results).
- **Consent to Turn On Location and Change Locating Method.** Check this check circle if you want to turn on location tracking and enable your phone to track its location via GPS and the cellular network.

- **Receive Notifications About Changes to the Weather.** Check this check circle if you want to get weather forecasts for your current location.

a. When you've made your choices on the *More Useful Features* screen, tap the *Finish* button.

Congratulations!

Your phone's setup is complete when the previous 12 steps are complete.

4

Find Your Way Around the Main Screens

Once you've completed the setup process, the lock screen normally appears. Once you unlock your phone using the unlock method you specified (see the next section), the *Home* screen appears. If you've used Android before on another device, you're probably ready to get started using your Galaxy S8, and you may not need to go through the rest of this chapter.

If you haven't been using Android, or if you'd like a quick orientation anyway, continue with the rest of this chapter. We'll meet the *Home* screen, the *lock* screen, the *Apps* screen, the *Notification panel*, and the *Quick Settings Panel*. We'll also look at using *Airplane Mode* and *Silent Mode* and how to turn off and restart your phone.

Unlock the Lock Screen

For security, Android includes a *lock* screen that you need to unlock before using the Galaxy S8. The *lock* screen uses the unlock method you set up in the chapter entitled **Start the Galaxy S8** earlier. A typical Android *lock* screen on the Galaxy S8 is shown:

Unlock your phone by performing the unlocking action you set. For example, if you used your fingerprint as the unlock method, place the appropriate finger on the fingerprint scanner. Or if you set a PIN, swipe the lock icon up to display the numeric keypad, type the PIN, and then tap the **OK** button

below the 9 keys.

Once you unlock the *lock* screen, Android displays the *Home* screen if you've just started your Galaxy S8 for the first time. On subsequent unlocks, Android displays the screen you were using last, enabling you to get right back to what you were doing.

Home Screen

The *Home* screen is your starting point for using Android. From it, you can launch an app, start a Google search, display the *Apps* screen, or open the *Notification* panel or the *Quick Settings Panel*. If the *Home* screen contains folders, you can open those folders to reach their contents. A typical default

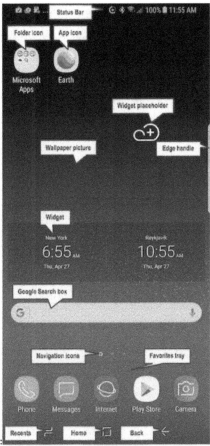

Android *Home* screen for the Galaxy S8 is shown:

Note: The *Home* screen typically has several panels that you can configure with the elements you find most useful. You navigate from panel to panel by swiping left or right across the screen.

These are the essential items you'll need for the *Home* screen:

- **Launch an app.** Tap an app icon, such as the *Play Store* icon, to launch the app. By putting your most-used apps on the *Home* screen, you can launch them quickly.
- **Start a Google search.** Tap in the *Google Search box* to start searching on the keywords you then type. Tap the *microphone* icon at the right end to search by voice.
- **Use the Favorites tray.** The *Favorites* tray is an area to which you can add the icons you want to have displayed on every panel of the *Home* screen. Put your key apps here so that you can launch them quickly.
- **Display the Apps screen.** Tap the *Apps* icon to display the *Apps* screen. We'll look at the *Apps* screen in the next section.
- **Open the Notification panel.** Pull down with one finger on the status bar at the top of the

screen to open the *Notification* panel. We'll look at the *Notification* panel a little later in this chapter.

- **Open the Quick Settings Panel.** Pull down with two fingers on the status bar at the top of the screen to open the *Quick Settings Panel*. We'll examine the *Quick Settings Panel* in a moment.
- **Open a folder.** If the *Home* screen contains one or more folders, you can tap a *folder* icon to display the contents of the folder. You can then tap the app you want to open. Folders enable you to group related items easily on the *Home* screen.

At the bottom of the screen are three soft buttons—looking from left to right, the **Recents** button, the **Home** button, and the **Back** button. The Galaxy S8 integrates these buttons into the screen, but in most apps they appear below the app's area of the screen. Here is how to use these three buttons:

- **Recents button:** Tap this button to display the *Recents* list, which enables you to jump straight to another running app.
- **Home button:** Tap this button to display the *Home* screen. If the Home screen panel that appears is not your starting panel, you can tap the **Home** button again to display the starting panel.
- **Back button:** Tap this button to go back to the previous screen. This screen may be in the same app or a different app. You can also tap the **Back** button to close a dialog box without making a choice in it.

Launch an App from the Apps Screen

As you saw in the previous section, you can quickly launch an app whose icon appears on the *Home* screen. The app's icon can be directly on the *Home* screen, in a folder on the *Home* screen, or in the *Favorites* tray.

For any app whose icon doesn't appear on the *Home* screen, use the *Apps* screen. Follow these steps:

1. Press the **Home** button to display the *Home* screen.

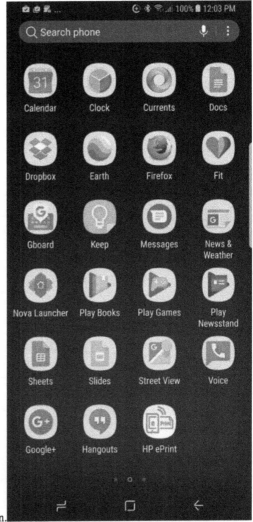

2. Swipe up or down to display the *Apps* screen.
3. If the app doesn't appear on the first *Apps* screen, scroll or swipe left until you see the app.
4. Tap the app's icon to launch the app.

Note: Android's formal name for the *Apps* screen is the *App drawer*. This book uses the term *"Apps screen"* because it seems easier to understand.

Work with the Notification Panel

When Android itself or an app that's permitted to raise notifications has something to communicate with you, the notification appears over the status bar at the top of the screen for a few seconds and then disappears.

To view your current crop of notifications, pull down with one finger on the left side of the status bar. The *Notification* panel opens, and you can work with your notifications like this:

- **Take an action with a notification.** Tap the action button on the notification. For example, on the notification for a missed phone call (such as in the screen here), you can tap the ***Call Back*** button to return the call or tap the ***Message*** button to send an instant message instead.
- **Display the app or feature that raised the notification:** Tap the notification.

- **Dismiss a notification:** Swipe the notification left or right off the list. This works with only some notifications; others remain on the *Notification* panel until you deal with them.
- **Clear all notifications:** Tap the ***Clear All*** button. If this button doesn't appear, the remaining notifications are ones that you can't clear.

Work with the Quick Settings Buttons and the Quick Settings Panel

The top part of the *Notification* panel contains three frequently used controls and two navigation buttons:

- **Settings button.** Tap this button to display the *Settings* app. This is often the most convenient way of getting to the *Settings* app.
- **Quick Settings Panel handle.** Drag this handle down to display the *Quick Settings Panel,* which we'll examine a little later in this chapter.
- **Quick Settings buttons.** The *Quick Settings* buttons are the row of buttons across the top of the *Notification* panel. You can tap one of these buttons to toggle a feature on or off or (if the feature has more complexity than just *On* and *Off)* to cycle through its settings.

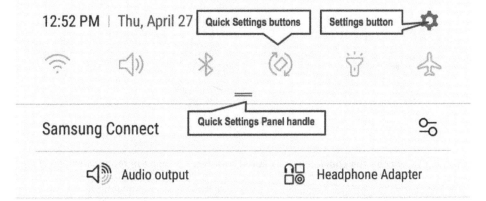

Tip: You can tap and hold a button on the *Quick Settings* buttons to jump straight to the associated screen in the *Settings* app. For example, tap and hold the *Wi-Fi* button to display the *Wi-Fi* screen, or tap and hold the *Sounds* icon (or the *Vibrate* icon, or the *Mute* icon, which appear in place of the *Sounds* icon when you turn on Vibrate or Mute) to display the *Sounds and Notifications* screen.

- **Samsung Connect.** Tap this button to start using the Samsung Connect feature to connect to nearby devices, such as your TV.

The*Quick Settings* buttons provide a handy group of frequently used controls, and you can customize them with your choice of buttons, as you'll see a little later in this chapter. But Android also provides the *Quick Settings Panel*, a larger area that gives you rapid access to a larger group of settings.

You can open the Quick Settings Panel in either of these ways:

- **From almost any screen.** Pull down with two fingers from the top of the screen. This move works from almost any screen, but there are some apps (especially games) that block this action.
- **From the Notification panel.** Drag the *Quick Settings Panel* handle down, or simply swipe

down.

Once you've opened the Quick Settings Panel, you can use most of its buttons like this:

- Tap an icon to toggle an item on or off or to cycle through its multiple states.
- Tap and hold an icon to display the associated screen in the *Settings* app.
- Tap an icon's label (the text below the icon) to display the *Quick Settings Panel* for the feature. For example, tap the *Performance Mode* label to display the *Performance Mode Quick Settings Panel*.

Customize the Quick Settings Bar and the Quick Settings Panel

Follow these steps to customize both the Quick Settings bar and the Quick Settings Panel:

1. Pull down from the top of the screen with two fingers to open the *Quick Settings Panel*.
2. Tap the **Menu** button (the three vertical dots in the upper-right corner of the *Quick Settings Panel*) to open the menu.
3. Tap the *Button Order* item on the menu to switch the *Quick Settings Panel* to *Edit Mode*.

4. Drag the icons into the order in which you want them. The first six icons are the ones that appear on the *Quick Settings bar*.
5. If you want to remove an icon you don't use, drag it to the gray area below the *Quick Settings Panel*.
6. To add an icon from the gray area, drag it to where you want it.
7. Tap the **Done** button when you finish.

5

Make the Most of Other Connections

Galaxy S8 includes several other means of connecting to other computers and devices:

- **NFC and Android Beam.** Near Field Communications (NFC) enables you to "beam" data from your phone to another NFC-enabled device and to make payments using the Tap and Pay system.
- **MirrorLink.** MirrorLink enables you to connect your phone to your car's system.
- **Download Booster.** Download Booster enables you to download large files faster by using both Wi-Fi and cellular connections.
- **VPN.** Virtual private networking (VPN) enables you to connect securely to another computer or network across the Internet.
- **Samsung Connect.** Samsung Connect is a Samsung technology for connecting quickly to other devices via wireless features such as Wi-Fi Direct and Miracast. Samsung Connect can be good for connecting to devices such as your printer, your speakers, and your TV. We'll look at the essentials of Samsung Connect in this chapter for general use (such as connecting to printers) and (for connecting to speakers and TV).
- **Printing.** You can print from your phone to a printer using several different technologies.

In this chapter, we'll look at these features. We'll also see how you can set your phone's default messaging app.

Transfer Data with NFC and Android Beam

Your Galaxy S8 includes an NFC chip for fast communication with other NFC-equipped devices. NFC is a handy technology that usually works pretty well, so you'll probably want to make the most of it.

Understand What NFC Is and What It's For

NFC is the abbreviation for Near Field Communications, a set of communication protocols that enable devices to communicate wirelessly at very short distances—usually just a few inches. When you bring two enabled NFC chips together, the chips detect each other's presence and attempt to establish communication.

Note: NFC was developed from Radio Frequency Identification (RFID) chips, which are widely used in industry for tasks such as identifying products using scanners.

To use the NFC chip on your Galaxy S8, you bring the back of the phone into immediate proximity with the NFC chip with which you're trying to establish communication. For example, you could touch a freestanding NFC chip to the back of your phone; or you could bring your phone and another NFC-enabled phone together back to back.

Your Galaxy S8 beeps when its NFC chip establishes communication with another chip, so you'll know when you're holding the chip or other device in the right place.

Turn On NFC on Your Galaxy S8

If NFC is turned off on your phone, you'll need to turn it on before you can use it.

Here's how to turn on NFC:

1. Open the *Settings* app.
2. Tap the **Connections** button to display the *Connections* screen.
3. Tap the main part of the *NFC and Payment* button (in other words, not the switch) to

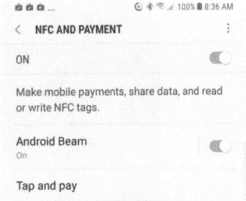

display the *NFC and Payment* screen.
4. Set the switch at the top of the screen to *On*.
5. If you want to be able to use the Android Beam feature for beaming data from one device to another, tap the**Android Beam** button to display the *Android Beam* screen, and then set the master switch to *On*.
6. If you want to use the Tap and Pay feature, tap the ***Tap and Pay*** button to display the *Tap and Pay* screen. Here, you can configure your installed payment service apps and service

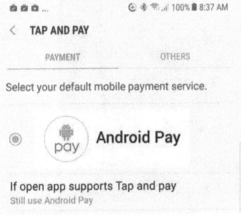

apps.

Note: You must install a payment service app, such as Google's Android Pay or Samsung's Samsung Pay, before you can set options on the *Tap and Pay* screen.

Transfer Data with NFC and Android Beam

Here's the easiest way to transfer data using NFC and Android Beam:

1. Open the file you want to transfer. For example, if you want to transfer a photo, open the Gallery app and then open the photo in it.

2. Bring your Galaxy S8 back to back with the destination device so that the NFC chips connect. You'll hear a beep when the chips connect. On your phone, the open item (the photo in our example) zooms much smaller, and the *Touch to Beam* prompt appears at the top of

the screen.

3. Tap the *Touch to Beam* prompt. Android transfers the file to the destination device and

displays a *File Sent* readout briefly to let you know it has done so.

You can also transfer a file via NFC by using the Share panel. This transfer method is especially useful when you are working in a file-management app, such as the My Files app that Samsung provides with many of its devices, but you can use it from any app that gives you access to the Share panel.

Here's how to transfer a file via NFC from the Share panel:

1. Select the file or files in the app, and then tap the **Share** button to display the *Share* panel.
2. Swipe left or right as needed until you see the Android Beam icon.

3. Tap the *Android Beam* icon. Android displays the *Touch Another Device with This Device to Share the Content* prompt.
4. Bring your phone back to back with the destination device. When the devices are in the right place relative to each other, your device plays a tone, and Android transfers the file or files.

Note: See the section Write a Wi-Fi Network's Details to an NFC Tag for instructions on storing the name and security details (such as the password) for a Wi-Fi network on an NFC chip so that you can share the details easily and securely with others—for example, to let your friends use your Wi-Fi network without telling them the password.

6

Set Up Printing and Print Documents

Android enables you to print documents quickly and easily from your phone to compatible printers. Before you can print, you may need to configure a print service plug-in such as the Samsung Print Service Plugin.

Understand the Main Ways of Printing from Your Phone

There are three main ways of printing from your phone:

- **Directly to a printer.** You can print via Wi-Fi (or, in some cases, Bluetooth) to a printer that accepts input this way.
- **To a printer via a computer.** If your printer can't accept input directly from your phone, you can make your desktop or laptop computer receive the print job and pass it along to the printer.
- **To a printer via the Internet.** You can register your printer with an Internet printing service such as Google's Cloud Print. Your phone then sends the print job across the Internet to Google's servers, which send it back to the printer.

Note: Cloud printing does work fine, but it's inherently absurd if the phone and printer are close to each other. Cloud printing may also represent a security risk, particularly for sensitive documents.

Make Your Printer Available to Your Phone

If your printer doesn't directly support printing from Android, you can use a third-party solution to share the printer attached to your computer. For example, you can install an app such as the PrinterShare Print Service app on the phone and then share your printer to make it available. On Windows, you install the PrinterShare app to share the printer; on the Mac, you simply turn on Printer Sharing in the Sharing pane in the System Preferences app.

Install and Configure the Samsung Print Service Plugin

If you want to print to one of your own printers from your phone, first try the Samsung Print Service Plugin. You may find this plug-in preinstalled on your phone; if not, you can quickly install it.

Open the Printing Screen in the Settings App

The Printing screen is where overall printing options can be configured for your phone. You will need to access this screen from time to time to make adjustments to your printing configurations.

Follow these steps to open the Printing screen:

1. Open the *Settings* app. For example, swipe up or down on the *Home* screen, and then tap the **Settings** icon on the Apps screen.
2. Tap the **Connections** button to display the *Connections* screen.
3. Tap the **More Connection Settings** button to display the *More Connection Settings* screen.

4. Tap the **Printing** button to display the *Printing* screen.

Look to see which print service plug-ins are installed. In the example provided, only Cloud Print is installed.

Install a Printing Plug-In

If the print plug-in you need doesn't appear on the Printing screen, it will need to be installed. This example uses the Samsung Print Service Plugin.

Follow these steps to install the Samsung Print Service plugin:

1. On the *Printing* screen in the Settings app, tap the **Download Plug-In** button.

Download plug-in

2. The *Print from Your Device* screen in the Play Store app appears, displaying a list of print plug-

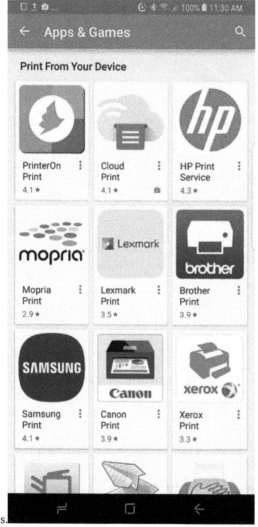

ins.

3. Tap the icon for the *Samsung Print Service* plug-in. The *Samsung Print Service Plugin* details

screen appears.

4. Tap the **Install** button. The Play Store app downloads and installs the plugin.

5. Now tap the **Recents** button to display the *Recents* screen, and tap the *Settings* thumbnail to return to the *Printing* screen, which now shows the plug-in you installed as shown:

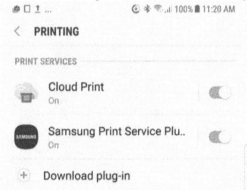

Configure a Print Plug-In

Printing plugins need to be configured once installed. The example provided uses the *Samsung Print*

Service Plugin, but the steps are similar for other plug-ins.

Follow these steps to configure a print plugin:

1. On the *Printing* screen, tap the main part of the plug-in's button (in other words, not the switch)

   to display the plug-in's screen.
2. If the switch at the top is set to *Off*, set it to *On*. The plug-in then begins searching for printers.

Note: If the search finishes without finding the printer, try tapping the **Menu** button (the three vertical dots) and then tapping the Search item on the menu to search again.

3. Tap the printer you want to use.

Tip: If you don't see the printer you want to use, verify that your phone is connected to the right Wi-Fi network.

4. Tap the **Menu** button (the three vertical dots) to open the menu, and then tap the *Printing Settings* item to display the settings screen for the plug-in.

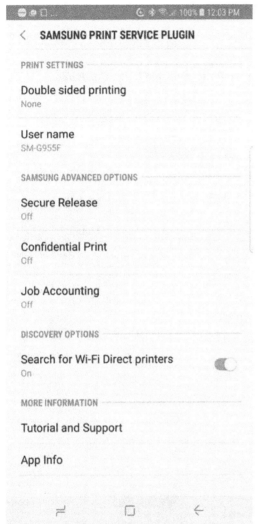

5. Choose settings as needed. For example, for the plug-in shown, you can enable double-side printing.
6. Tap the < button in the upper-left corner of the screen or the **Back** button below the screen when you finish configuring the plug-in.

Print a Document

After setting up your printers, you can print to them. In some apps, you give the Print command from the menu or from the navigation panel. In other apps, you give the Share command and then select the appropriate printing plug-in as the destination for sharing.

Print a Document Using the Print Command

The print command provides a straight-forward way to print most images and documents being viewed on your Galaxy S8.

Follow these steps to print an email using the Print command in the Gmail app:

1. Navigate to your Gmail account and view the contents of any message.

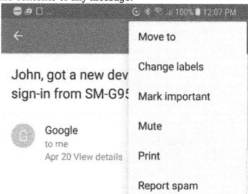

2. Tap the **Menu** button to display the menu.
3. Tap the **Print** item to display the Print screen.

4. If the document has multiple pages, you can tap the yellow circle containing a check mark at the lower-right corner of a page if you don't want to print that page.

5. If you need to change the printing options, tap the down-arrow (v) button at the top of the printing panel. The *Printing panel* expands, and you can choose the options you need.

6. When you're ready to print, tap the **Print** button (the yellow circle with the printer icon) at the right side of the top of the document.

Print a Document Using the Share Command

Another method to print from the Galaxy S8 involves using the Share command. This can be used as a quick way to print images and documents on your phone. It can be accessed by selecting the Share icon when an image or document is selected. Here's an example of printing using the Share command in the Gallery app:

Follow these steps to print a document using the Share command:

1. Tap the screen to display the control buttons.
2. Tap the **Share** icon to display the Share panel.

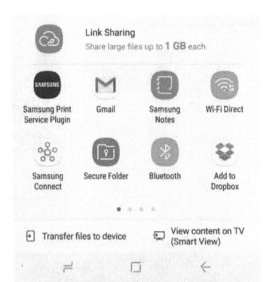

Link Sharing
Share large files up to 1 GB each.

Samsung Print Service Plugin	**Gmail**	**Samsung Notes**	**Wi-Fi Direct**
Samsung Connect	**Secure Folder**	**Bluetooth**	**Add to Dropbox**

Transfer files to device   View content on TV (Smart View)

3. Tap the appropriate print plug-in. The *Select a Printer* screen appears.

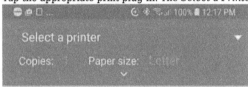

4. Tap the **Select a Printer** pop-up button to display the *Select a Printer* panel.

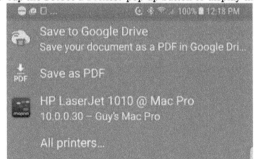

5. If you don't want to print any of the document's pages, tap the yellow circle containing a check mark at the lower-right corner of a page to deselect the appropriate pages.

6. If you need to change the printing options, tap the down-arrow **(v)** button at the bottom of the printing panel. The *Printing panel* expands, and you can choose the options you need.

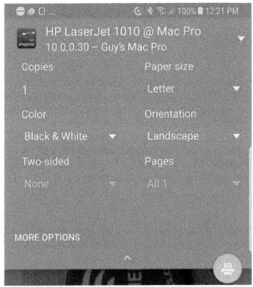

7. Tap the **Print** button (the yellow circle with the printer icon) to print the document.

7

Understand and Use MirrorLink

Your Galaxy S8 includes a feature called MirrorLink for connecting the phone to your vehicle's information and entertainment system. Once you've connected the phone, you can use the information and entertainment system's head unit to control apps on the phone. For example, you can use the head unit to play music from your phone through the car's stereo or to control phone calls.

Note: MirrorLink is relatively little used as of this writing. This section explains the essentials of MirrorLink in case you have the opportunity to use it, but it to save space it points you to sections in different chapters for parts of the process rather than duplicating the instructions here.

Which Cars Support MirrorLink?

To use MirrorLink with your phone, your car's information and entertainment system must support version 1.1 or a later version of the MirrorLink standard. You can find a partial list of MirrorLink-enabled cars at the MirrorLink website (Partial List of MirrorLink-Enabled Cars).

If you have one of these models of car, check its specifications to find out whether it supports MirrorLink version 1.1 or a later version. If so, you're in business. If not, consider getting a MirrorLink-enabled car stereo unit. Most of these cost several hundred dollars and involve removing your car's existing unit, but even if you have to pay for labor, that's much less than buying a new car.

Connect Your Phone to Your Car's System Using MirrorLink

To get MirrorLink working between your phone and your car's head unit, you must first pair the two devices via Bluetooth.

Note: The first time you connect your phone to your car's head unit, your phone must be connected to the cellular network.

Here is a brief summary of the steps for connecting:

1. Enable Bluetooth on the head unit.
2. Enable Bluetooth on your phone.
3. On your phone, display the *Bluetooth* screen in the *Settings* app. Doing this makes the phone visible via Bluetooth.
4. On the head unit, display the Bluetooth screen and scan for devices. Your phone should appear.
5. On the head unit, tap the item for your phone, and then follow the prompts to establish the pairing.

Note: To enable the MirrorLink head unit to control your phone via USB, you must go into the Developer options on the phone and enable USB debugging for the head unit.

Enable the Download Booster Feature

The Download Booster feature lets you get faster download speeds by using both the cellular connection and a Wi-Fi connection for transferring files larger than 30MB. If your data plan has some spare capacity in a typical month, you'll likely want to enable Download Booster so that you can get large files more quickly.

Here's how to turn on the Download Booster feature:

1. Open the *Settings* app.
2. Tap the **Connections** button to display the *Connections* screen.
3. Tap the **More Connection Settings** button to display the **More Connection Settings** screen.
4. Set the *Download Booster* switch to *On*.

Note: Tap the main part of the **Download Booster** button (in other words, not the switch) if you want to see the *Download Booster* screen, which contains an explanation of Download Booster.

Once you've enabled Download Booster, it kicks in when you go to download a file larger than 30MB.

8

Communicate Securely via VPN

Your Galaxy S8 enables you to use a technology called virtual private network (VPN for short) or virtual private networking (also VPN for short) to communicate securely across the Internet. A virtual private network uses encryption to establish a secure connection between your phone and the destination computer.

Understand What VPN Is Useful For

Of the many reasons to use a VPN, these three reasons are probably the most common:

- **Security.** You can use a VPN to connect securely to the computer network at your workplace from your home or elsewhere. Many companies, organizations, and government bodies insist that employees use virtual private networking when connecting to their networks from outside the network.
- **Protecting your communications data.** Without encryption, government agencies and regulatory bodies can examine your communications data and see in great detail what you have been doing on the Internet. Encryption via VPN makes this kind of intrusion far harder, though in most cases not impossible.
- **Hiding or changing your geographical location.** You can use a VPN to hide your real geographical location by making your computer appear to be in a different location. This feature of VPN can benefit anyone from investigative journalists and whistleblowers through to people who want to use services that use geographical restrictions (sometimes called geo-blocking). For example, some video-streaming services are available only in the U.S.A.; by using a VPN, you can make your computer appear to be in the U.S.A. so that you can access such services.

Note: Using a VPN is legal in most places as of this writing. Some countries, including France and Saudi Arabia, place restrictions on the use of encryption, discouraging the use of VPNs.

Set Up a VPN Connection on Your Phone

When you need a VPN connection, get the details from the VPN provider or systems administrator. Here's what you need to know:

- **VPN Type.** The type describes the technology the VPN uses, such as PPTP or L2TP/IPSec PSK.
- **Server Address.** The address can be a hostname, such as vpn1.notionalpress.com, or an IP address, such as 50.7.63.17.
- **Security Information.** This depends on the VPN type. For example, for an L2TP VPN, you may need the L2TP secret; for an IPSec VPN, you may need the IPSec pre-shared key.
- **Login Information.** For many VPN types, you'll need your login name and password. For others, you may need a digital certificate, a piece of encrypted information that verifies your device's identity.

Understanding VPN Terms

VPNs use lots of technical terms. You likely don't need to understand all of them, but you may find these essentials helpful.

- PPTP is the abbreviation for Point-to-Point Tunneling Protocol. PPTP is an older VPN technology that's not entirely secure, but it's still widely used.
- L2TP is the abbreviation for Layer 2 Tunneling Protocol. L2TP is generally regarded as more secure than PPTP, has been around for a while, and is widely used.
- IPSec is the abbreviation for Internet Protocol Security. IPSec comes in different flavors but overall provides strong security.
- PSK is the abbreviation for Pre-Shared Key. The pre-shared key is a piece of information used to connect to the VPN. A pre-shared key is often a password or a passphrase, but it's sometimes a hexadecimal string. (Hexadecimal is base 16, using the numbers 0–9 and the letters A–F.)
- RSA is an encryption algorithm. The abbreviation comes from the first letter of the last name of its three creators, Rivest, Shamir, and Adelman.
- Xauth (usually pronounced ex-auth) is the acronym for Extended Authentication, a form of authentication used for IPSec connections.
- IKE (pronounced as the three letters rather than like the nickname for Eisenhower) is the abbreviation for Internet Key Exchange. IKE is a protocol used to exchange encryption keys to establish a secure connection.

Tip: Some VPN providers supply Android apps that establish and manage VPN connections for you. Such apps save you from having to set up your VPN connections manually, so it's well worth seeing if your VPN provider offers an app.

Armed with the information required for the VPN, follow these steps to set up the VPN on your phone:

1. Open the *Settings* app.
2. Tap the **Connections** button to display the *Connections* screen.
3. Tap the **More Connection Settings** button to display the *More Connection Settings* screen.

4. Tap the **VPN** button to display the VPN screen. Until you set up a VPN, this screen shows the

readout No VPNs in the middle.

5. Tap the **Add VPN** button in the upper-right corner of the screen to open the *Add VPN* dialog box.

Add VPN

Name
Work VPN

Type
L2TP/IPSec PSK ▼

Server address
us51.nordvpn.com

L2TP secret
Not used

IPSec identifier
Not used

IPsec pre-shared key
●●●●●●●●●●

○ Show advanced options

Username
h85466

Password
●●●●●●●●●●●●●●●●|

○ Always-on VPN

CANCEL   SAVE

6. Tap the *Name* field and type a descriptive name for the VPN, such as "Work" or "Virtual U.S.A.".

7. Tap the *Type* pop-up menu and then tap the *VPN* type. Your choices are PPTP, L2TP/IPSec PSK, L2TP/IPSec RSA, IPSec Hybrid RSA, IPSec Xauth PSK, IPSec Xauth RSA, IPSec IKEv2 PSK, or IPSec IKEv2 RSA. The fields in the lower part of the Add VPN dialog box change to match the VPN type you select.

8. Tap the *Server Address* field and type the hostname (such as vpn1.notionalpress.com) or IP address (such as 50.7.63.17) for the VPN server.

9. Fill in any authentication information needed for the VPN. For example, for an L2TP/IPSec PSK VPN, tap the *IPSec Pre-Shared Key* field and type the pre-shared key.

10. Select the *Always-On VPN* check circle if you want the VPN to be on all the time.

11. When you finish adding the information for the VPN, tap the *Save* button to save the VPN. The VPN created the appears on the *VPN screen* under the name you specified.

Use a VPN Connection on Your Phone

After setting up one or more VPN connections on your phone, you can quickly connect to a VPN. The first time you connect to a VPN, you provide your authentication information, such as your user name and password. You can choose to store this information for future use or (for greater security) opt to enter the information each time you connect to the VPN.

Follow these steps to use a VPN connection:

1. Display the VPN screen in the *Settings* app. (Open the *Settings* app, tap the **More Connection Settings** button, and then tap the **VPN** button.)
2. Tap the button for the VPN you want to use. The *Connect To* dialog box opens, showing the VPN's name—for example, if the VPN is named "Work VPN", the dialog box is called *Connect to Work*

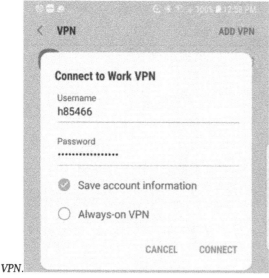

VPN.

Note: This example is for an L2TP VPN. For other VPN types, you may need to provide other authentication information.

3. Type your user name in the *Username* field.
4. Tap the *Password* field and type your password.
5. Check the *Save Account Information* check box if you want to store the information for future use. Doing so enables you to start using the VPN more quickly next time.
6. Tap the **Connect** button. Your phone establishes the VPN connection, and the *Connected* readout

appears on the VPN's button on the VPN screen.

Note: The key icon on the left of the status bar indicates that your phone is connected to a VPN.

After connecting to the VPN, you can access items on the VPN much as if you were connected to the network from within it. For example, after connecting to your work network via VPN, you can access your e-mail, your files, and shared resources (depending on what the administrator permits VPN users to do).

When you finish using the VPN, disconnect from it like this:

1. Open the *Notification* panel.
2. Tap the *VPN Is Activated* notification to display the dialog box for that VPN.

3. Tap the ***Disconnect*** button. Your phone disconnects the VPN connection.

Set Your Phone's Default Messaging App

The Galaxy S8 usually include two or more messaging apps, such as these two:

- **Messages.** Samsung's Messages app is a straightforward messaging app that's easy to use. Messages ties in with some of the Samsung apps you're likely to find on your phone, giving you an easy way to send messages from those apps.
- **Hangouts.** Google's Hangouts app includes messaging among many other capabilities, including making audio and video calls across the Internet.

To avoid confusion, it's a good idea to tell your Galaxy S8 which messaging app you want to use as the default.

Note: The default messaging app is the app that Android uses when you take, from another app, an action that involves creating an instant message.

Here's how to set the default messaging app:

1. Open the *Settings* app.
2. Tap the **Apps** button to display the *Apps* screen.
3. Tap the **Menu** button (the three vertical dots) to open the menu.
4. Tap the *Default Apps* item on the menu to display the *Default Apps* screen.

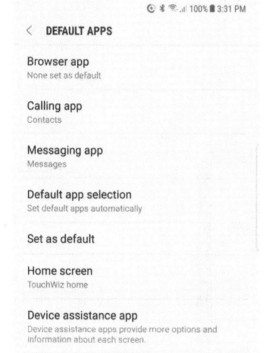

5. Tap the **Messaging App** button to display the *Messaging App* screen.

⊕ ✱ 📶 100% 🔋 3:31 PM

< **MESSAGING APP**

Select your default messaging app.

○ 🔲 Messages

○ 💬 Messenger

○ 💬 Hangouts

◉ 💬 Messages

6. Tap the **option** button for the app you want to use as the default—for example, *Messages*. The *Default Apps* screen then appears again.

Note: If you select an app other than *Messages* as your default messaging app, Android displays the *Change Messaging* App dialog box, warning you that you will not be able to use some features of Samsung apps with the app you have chosen. Tap the **OK** button if you want to proceed with the change; otherwise, tap the **Cancel** button.

Tip: While you're on the *Default Applications* screen, you may want to check the settings for the other default apps—*Browser App, Calling App, Home Screen*, and *Device Assistance* app—and change them if necessary. If you want your phone to check with you before setting a default app, tap the **Default App Selection** button and then tap the *Ask Before Setting Default Apps* item in the pop-up menu.

9

Connect, Use, and Manage Bluetooth Devices

Your Galaxy S8 includes the Bluetooth technology for connecting peripheral devices without cables. Bluetooth is great for devices such as headphones and headsets, speakers, and keyboards. This chapter shows you how to set up Bluetooth devices with your Galaxy S8, use them, and manage them.

Turn Bluetooth On and Off

The quick way to turn Bluetooth on or off is by using the Quick Settings bar at the top of the Notification panel or by using the Quick Settings Panel.

Follow these steps to toggle Bluetooth On and Off using the Notification panel:

1. Pull down from the top of the screen to open the *Notification* panel.

2. Tap the **Bluetooth** button ⁎ (the third button from the left here) to toggle Bluetooth on or off.

Note: You can also turn Bluetooth on or off by by setting the Bluetooth switch on the Bluetooth Quick Settings Panel or by setting the On/Off switch at the top of the Bluetooth screen in the Settings app.
Tip: Turn Bluetooth off when you're not using it. This not only saves you battery power but also helps you avoid receiving unwanted advertising via Bluetooth.

Display the Bluetooth Quick Settings Panel and the Bluetooth Screen

To work with Bluetooth devices, you use the Bluetooth Quick Settings Panel and the Bluetooth screen in the Settings app.

Display the Bluetooth Quick Settings Panel

Here's how to display the Bluetooth Quick Settings Panel:

1. Pull down from the top of the screen with two fingers to open the *Quick Settings Panel*.

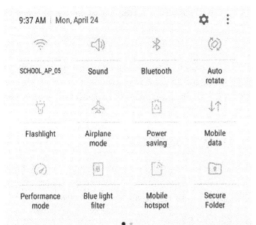

2. Tap the **Bluetooth** label (the actual text, not the icon). The *Bluetooth Quick Settings Panel* opens, showing any devices with which your Galaxy S8 is paired. (We'll get to pairing shortly.)

From the *Bluetooth Quick Settings Panel*, you can take four actions:

- **Turn Bluetooth on or off.** Set the Bluetooth switch to *On* or *Off*, as needed.
- **View your paired devices.** Look at the *Paired Devices* list.
- **Display the Bluetooth screen in the Settings app.** Tap the **Details** button.
- **Close the Bluetooth Quick Settings Panel.** Tap the **Done** button.

Display the Bluetooth Screen in the Settings App

You can display the Bluetooth screen in whichever of these ways you find convenient:

- Pull down from the top of the screen to open the *Notification* panel, and then tap and hold the **Bluetooth** button.
- Pull down from the top of the screen with two fingers to open the *Quick Settings Panel*, and then tap and hold the **Bluetooth** icon.
- Pull down from the top of the screen with two fingers to open the *Quick Settings Panel*, tap the **Bluetooth** label to display the *Bluetooth Quick Settings Panel*, and then tap the **Details** button.
- Open the *Settings* app, tap the **Connections** button, and then tap the **Bluetooth** button on the *Connections* screen.

Pair a Bluetooth Device with Your Galaxy S8

To use a Bluetooth device with your Galaxy S8, you must first pair the device with the phone. Pairing is a sort of formal introduction that tells the two pieces of kit that you want them to be able to connect. Pairing helps ensure that unauthorised Bluetooth devices can't connect to your phone.

Follow these steps to pair a device with your Galaxy S8:

1. Get the Bluetooth device ready. Charge it if necessary.
2. Display the *Bluetooth* screen in the *Settings* app in one of the ways explained in the previous

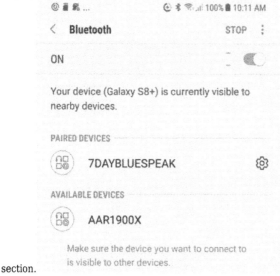

   section.
3. Set the switch at the top of the screen to the *On* position if it is set to *Off* currently. Android automatically starts scanning for available Bluetooth devices within range. You can stop the scan by tapping the **Stop** button above the switch at the top of the screen.
4. Set the Bluetooth device to Pairing mode. How you do this depends on the device, but usually it involves a sustained or complex button press. Most devices give some kind of indication when you get this right, such as flashing a blue light or alternating flashes of a blue light and a red light.

Tip: If Android has stopped scanning for Bluetooth devices by the time you set the Bluetooth device to Pairing mode, tap the Scan button to start scanning again. The Scan button appears in place of the Stop button when Android is not scanning.

5. Tap the device's entry in the Available Devices list on the Galaxy S8.
6. For some devices, the *Bluetooth Pairing Request* dialog box opens. Type the code on the keyboard and press **Enter** or tap the **OK** button, depending on the device you're connecting.
7. When the device appears in the *Paired Devices* list, you can start using it if *Connected* appears on the button. Normally, Android connects the device automatically after pairing succeeds.

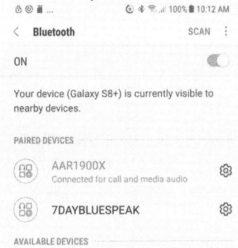

Configure a Paired Bluetooth Device

After pairing a Bluetooth device with your Galaxy S8, you can configure the paired device to make it work the way you want it to. As you'd expect, the configuration options available depend on the device and what it does. But at the very minimum, you can change the name used for the device from the default name to a name that's easier to identify.

Follow these steps to configure a paired Bluetooth device:

1. Access the *Paired Devices* list screen using the methods described previously.
2. Tap the **Settings** icon (the gear icon) to the right of the device's name in the *Paired Devices* list on the *Bluetooth* screen. The *Paired Device* screen appears as shown:

3. To rename the device, tap the **Rename** button, type the new name (preferably something descriptive) in the *Rename* dialog box, and then tap the **Rename** button.
4. To choose which roles you can use the device for, go to the *Use For* list, and set each switch to *On* or *Off*, as needed. For example, for the keyboard shown here, you can set the *Text Input* switch to *On* or *Off*. Normally, you'd want to set the *Text Input* switch to *On*, because a Bluetooth keyboard isn't much use if you can't type text on it.
5. For an audio device, you get switches such as the *Call Audio* switch and the *Media Audio* switch,

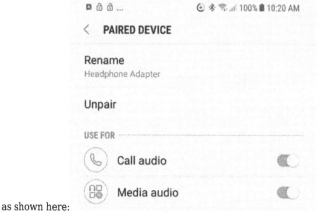

as shown here:

Connect and Disconnect Bluetooth Devices

After you've paired a Bluetooth device, you can connect it by tapping its button in the Paired Devices list on the Bluetooth screen. Connecting the device normally takes a few seconds. The Paired Devices list shows the names of connected devices in blue with brief details, such as Connected as input device or Connected for call audio; the names of devices that are not connected appear in black.

Follow these steps to start using a paired device:

1. Access the *Bluetooth Quick Settings Panel* using the methods described earlier.
2. Tap the name of the device you would like to use.

3. The status of the device changes and is noted by "Connected..." text appearing under the name of the device as shown:

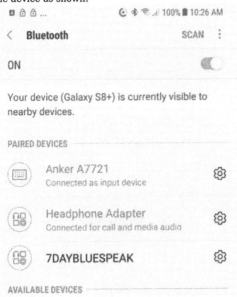

When you're ready to stop using a Bluetooth device for the time being, tap its button in the *Paired Devices* list. Android disconnects the device, and the *Connected* readout disappears from its button in the *Paired Devices* list. A pop-up message appears for a few seconds saying that the Bluetooth connection with the device has ended.

Follow these steps to stop using a paired device:

1. Access the *Bluetooth Quick Settings Panel* using the methods described earlier.
2. Tap the name of the device you would like to stop using.
3. A status indicator appears confirming the connection with the device has been ended as shown:

Unpair a Bluetooth Device

When you want to stop using a Bluetooth device permanently, unpair it from your phone. It is important to note that unpairing a device is different from disconnecting it, an unpaired device will no longer display in the list of paired devices will will still appear as an available device.

Follow these steps to unpair a Bluetooth device:

1. On the *Bluetooth* screen, tap the **Settings** icon (the gear icon) to the right of the device's name in the *Paired Devices* list. The *Paired Device* screen appears.
2. Tap the **Unpair** button. Android unpairs the device and displays the *Bluetooth* screen again, where it removes the device from the *Paired Devices* list. The device appears in the *Available*

Devices list so you can pair it again if necessary.

Play Audio Through Bluetooth Devices

Once you've paired and connected a Bluetooth speaker, you can play audio through it easily. To do so, follow these steps:

1. Pull down from the top of the screen to open the *Notification* panel.

2. In the *Samsung Connection* section, tap the *Audio Output* icon, the speaker icon on the left, to

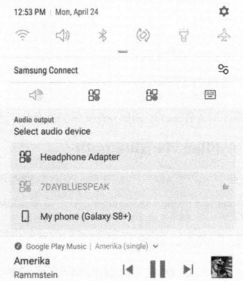

open the *Select Audio Device* pane.
3. Tap the output device you want to use.

The Galaxy S8 and Galaxy S8+ also have a special feature called Dual Audio that lets you play audio to two Bluetooth devices at the same time. This feature is great both when you need to use an extra speaker to crank up the volume to 11 and when you want to play audio in two nearby rooms at once. (Bluetooth has a limited range, so the rooms must be relatively close together.)

Here's how to use Dual Audio to play audio to two Bluetooth devices at once:

1. Connect the two devices as explained earlier in this chapter.
2. Pull down from the top of the screen to open the *Notification* panel.
3. Tap and hold the **Bluetooth** icon to display the *Bluetooth* screen in the *Settings* app.
4. Tap the **Menu** button (the three vertical dots) to open the menu.
5. Tap the **Dual Audio** item to display the *Dual Audio* screen.

> You can play sound from your phone to 2 different Bluetooth devices.
>
> The 2 connected devices may experience a slight difference in sound output.

6. Set the switch at the top of the screen to *On*.

Transfer Files via Bluetooth

Bluetooth can be a great way to transfer files between your Galaxy S8 and other devices.

Start by pairing your phone with the other device, as explained in the section *Pair a Bluetooth Device with Your Galaxy S8*, earlier in this chapter.

Send a File via Bluetooth

Once you've paired your phone with the device with which you want to share files, you can easily send files. Follow these steps:

1. Navigate to the file you want to share. For example, you might navigate to a photo in the *Gallery* app.
2. Give the *Share* command. For example, in the *Gallery* app, tap the **Share** button.

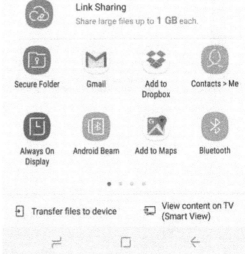

3. In the *Share* panel, tap the **Bluetooth** icon.
4. On the *Select Device* screen, tap the device to which you want to send the file. Your phone contacts the device and, if the device returns an acceptance of the file, sends the file. Your phone displays the File sent pop-up message briefly to confirm that it has sent the file.

Receive a File via Bluetooth

Receiving a file via Bluetooth is even easier than sending one. Follow these general steps:

---

1. When the *File Transfer* dialog box opens, look at the From readout (which shows the device), the File Name readout, and the *Size* readout, and decide whether to accept the transfer. If so, tap the **Accept** button; if not, tap the **Decline** button.

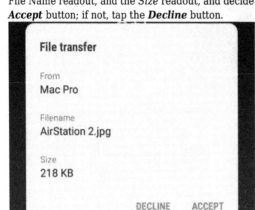

2. Pull down from the top of the screen with one finger to open the *Notification* panel.

3. Tap the *File Received* notification to display the *Inbound Transfers* screen.

4. Tap the button for the file you've to open it in a suitable app (assuming your phone has one).

Troubleshoot Bluetooth Connections

Bluetooth is great when it works, but it can be sullen and balky. You may have trouble pairing devices, or you may find that Android drops Bluetooth connections for no reason.

1. Turn Bluetooth Off and Then On Again on Your Galaxy S8

If Bluetooth isn't working properly on your Galaxy S8, the first troubleshooting move is to turn Bluetooth off and then on again. You can turn it off and on in any of these ways:

- **Notification panel.** Tap the ***Bluetooth*** button to turn Bluetooth off, wait a second or two, and then tap the ***Bluetooth*** button again to turn Bluetooth on again.
- **Quick Settings Panel.** You can perform the same maneuver in the *Quick Settings Panel*: Tap the *Bluetooth* button to turn Bluetooth off, wait a second, and then tap the ***Bluetooth*** button again.
- **Bluetooth Quick Settings Panel.** Set the Bluetooth switch to *Off*, wait for a second or two, and then set the Bluetooth switch to *On*.
- **Bluetooth screen in the Settings app.** Set the switch at the top to *Off*, wait a few seconds, and then set the switch to *On*.

2. Turn Bluetooth Off and Then On Again on the Other Device

Depending on the device you're trying to use, you might want to try turning Bluetooth off and on again for that device too. If the device doesn't have a way of turning Bluetooth on and off, turn the device itself off and then back on.

3. Restart Your Galaxy S8

If Bluetooth is still uncooperative, restart the Galaxy S8 device. This takes a couple of minutes, but it can clear up any number of tedious problems, so don't shirk it.

Tip: It's also worth updating your Galaxy S8 to the latest version of Android if you haven't already done so.

10

Configure the Accessibility Settings You Need

Your Galaxy S8 provides a wide range of accessibility settings to make the phone easier to use. The accessibility settings fall into three main categories:

- **Vision**. These options are designed to help those with vision problems. For example, the Voice Assistant feature can announce the items on screen if you cannot see them.
- **Hearing.** These options are intended to help those with hearing problems. For example, the Flash Notification feature can flash the camera light to let you know you have receive notifications.
- **Dexterity and Interaction.** These options can help make your device easier to use with your fingers and hands.

Beyond these major categories, the Accessibility screen includes other settings that include unlocking the screen with a series of swipes, gaining direct access to specific settings and functions, and answering and ending calls.

Display the Accessibility Screen

To start configuring accessibility options, display the Accessibility screen in the Settings app.

Follow these steps:

1. Open the *Settings* app. For example, swipe up or down on the *Home* screen, and then tap the **Settings** icon on the *Apps* screen.
2. Tap the **Accessibility** button toward the bottom of the *Settings* screen.

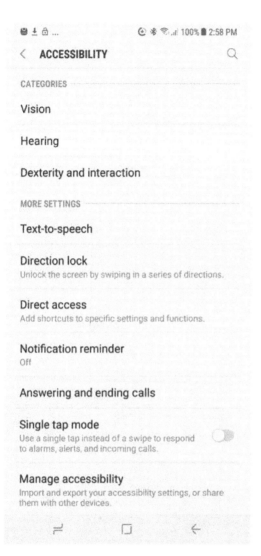

CATEGORIES

Vision

Hearing

Dexterity and interaction

MORE SETTINGS

Text-to-speech

Direction lock
Unlock the screen by swiping in a series of directions.

Direct access
Add shortcuts to specific settings and functions.

Notification reminder
Off

Answering and ending calls

Single tap mode
Use a single tap instead of a swipe to respond
to alarms, alerts, and incoming calls.

Manage accessibility
Import and export your accessibility settings, or share
them with other devices.

Choose Vision Options

Perform this step to access the vision options:

1. Tap the **Vision** button at the top of the *Accessibility* screen to display the *Vision* screen. At first, it looks like the screen provided below, with most of the controls disabled because *Voice Assistant* is

off.

These are the Vision options you can set for accessibility:

- **Voice Assistant.** Tap this button to display the Voice Assistant screen. Here, you can set the switch to On to turn on Voice Assistant, which announces items on screen. If you turn on Voice Assistant, tap the Settings button to display the Voice Assistant Settings screen, and then configure Voice Assistant to work the way you prefer. When you finish, tap the < button in the upper-left corner of the screen or the Back button below the screen twice to return to the Vision

‹　VOICE ASSISTANT SETTINGS

Speech volume
Match media volume

Text-to-speech

Pitch changes
Set voice feedback to use a different pitch when
you're entering text with the keyboard.

Read keyboard input aloud
Always

Speak while screen off
Read notifications aloud while the screen is off.

Mute with proximity sensor
Mute voice feedback when the proximity sensor
is covered.

Shake for continuous reading
Off

Read caller ID aloud

Phonetic alphabet
When reading letters aloud, use the
corresponding word from the phonetic alphabet
instead of the letter name.

Usage hints
Read usage hints aloud after a brief delay when

⇄　　　　　▢　　　　←

screen.

- **Dark Screen.** Set this switch to On if you want to keep the screen turned off. You'd normally turn on Dark Screen because you can't see the screen and you want to prevent others from seeing what the screen is showing. You can toggle Dark Screen on and off by double-pressing the Power button.
- **Rapid Key Input.** Set this switch to On if you want to use the Rapid Input feature. With Voice Assistant on but with Rapid Key Input switched off, you slide your finger across the keyboard until Voice Assistant announces the character you want to type; you then double-tap the character to type it. With Rapid Key Input switched on, you slide your finger across the keyboard until Voice Assistant announces the character you want to type; you then lift your finger from the keyboard to type the character. You'll likely want to experiment with Rapid Key Input to see if you find it

helpful.

- **Speak Passwords.** Set this switch to On if you want Voice Assistant to speak each password character you type. You'll want to make sure nobody can overhear you—for example, by using headphones.
- Accessibility Shortcut. Set this switch to On to enable the Accessibility Shortcut feature. Tap the button to display the Accessibility Shortcut screen if you want to see a fuller explanation of the feature. Once you've enabled Accessibility Shortcut, you can turn on accessibility features by pressing and holding the Power button until you feel a vibration or your phone plays a sound, and then pressing and holding with two fingers until the phone announces that the features have been turned on.
- **Voice Label.** Tap this button to display the Voice Label screen. Here, you can record your voice (or someone else's voice) announcing the names of objects you want to identify. Tap the Done button when you're satisfied with a recording, then hold an NFC chip to the back of your phone to write to the chip a reference to the recording. You can subsequently identify the object by bringing your phone to the NFC chip.

Note: Voice labels on NFC tags are specific to your phone. Your phone doesn't actually write the voice label to the NFC tag—instead, the phone writes a coded reference on the tag that enables the phone to replay the voice label you record. So if you touch another phone to the NFC tag, you will not hear the voice label you recorded.

- **Screen Zoom and Font.** Tap this button to display the full-screen dialog box shown next. You can then set the Larger Font Sizes switch to On; drag the Screen Zoom switch along the Small-Large axis to set the zoom; and drag the Font Size slider along the Tiny-Extra Huge axis to set the font size. In the Font Style section, you can choose a different font style for system text.

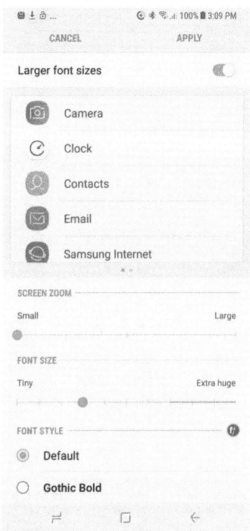

Tap the Apply button when you finish.

- **High Contrast Fonts.** Set this switch to On if you want to increase the contrast between fonts and the backgrounds on which they appear.
- **High Contrast Keyboard.** Set this switch to On if you want to make the keyboard more visible.
- **Show Button Shapes.** Set this switch to On if you want your phone to display a shaded background around buttons to make them easier to identify.
- **Magnifier Window.** Tap this button to display the Magnifier Window screen. Here, you can set the switch at the top to On to enable the Magnifier Window feature. The Magnifier Window then appears, and you can drag it around the screen as needed; tap the X button in the upper-right corner when you want to close it. With the Magnifier Window feature enabled, you can use the Zoom Percentage slider to set the amount of zoom. You can also tap the Magnifier Size button to

display the Magnifier Size dialog box, in which you can tap the Small option button, the Medium option button, or the Large option button to set the size of the Magnifier Window.

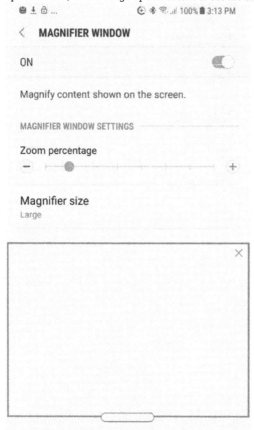

Note: Turning on the Magnifier Window feature disables the following other accessibility options if they are enabled: Voice Assistant, Reduce Screen Size, Assistant Menu, Interaction Control, Universal Switch, Magnification Gestures, and Always On Display.

- **Magnification Gestures.** Set this switch to On to enable yourself to use gestures to magnify part of the screen. Once you've enabled the Magnification Gestures feature, triple-tap to zoom in. You can then pan around by placing on the screen and dragging them. You can pinch inward or outward to change the zoom level. When you are done using Magnification Gestures, triple-tap to zoom out again.

Note: To see more detail on Magnification Gestures, tap the main part of the*Magnification Gestures* button and read the explanation on the *Magnification Gestures* screen.

- **Large Mouse/Touchpad Pointer.** Set this switch to On to increase the size of the pointer that appears when you connect a mouse or a touchpad.

- **Grayscale.** Set this switch to On to change the display to grayscale.
- **Negative Colors.** Set this switch to On to invert the colors on screen, like this. Inverting the colors can make the screen easier to see in certain lighting conditions or with certain eye

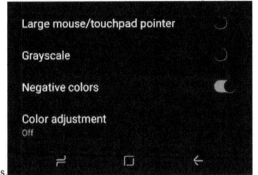

conditions.
- **Color Adjustment.** Tap this button to display the Color Adjustment screen, and then set the switch at the top to On. An screen appears containing explanatory text. Tap the Start button. On the screen that appears, tap the colored squares in the middle of the screen in order to move them to the smaller, empty squares at the bottom, arranging the colors in order of similarity. Then tap the Done button.

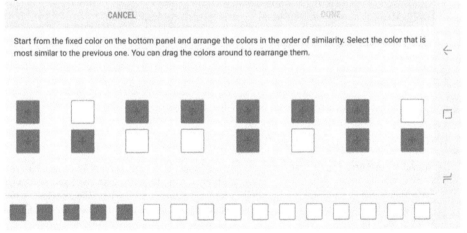

Choose Hearing Options

Android and the Galaxy S8 offer hearing settings that can be tailored to your specific needs including those of the hearing impaired.

Follow these steps to set hearing options:

1. Tap the **Hearing** button in the *Categories* list at the top of the *Accessibility* screen to display the

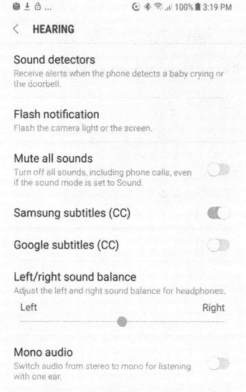

Hearing screen.

These are the options you can set on the Hearing screen:

- **Sound Detectors.** Tap this button to display the Sound Detectors screen. Here, you can set the Baby Crying Detector switch to On to use the Baby Crying Detector feature or set the Doorbell Detector switch to on to use the Doorbell Detector feature. If you turn on the Doorbell Detector, the Record Doorbell Sound screen appears, enabling you to record the sound for the doorbell you want to monitor.

Caution: The Baby Crying Detector feature and Doorbell Detector feature are interesting and well-intended experiments, but you should read all the warnings carefully before trying them.

The Baby Crying Detector feature requires you to place your phone within 1 meter of the baby and with no background noise. Similarly, the Doorbell Detector feature wants you to place your phone within 3 meters of the doorbell and with no background noise. Enabling either of these features also turns off *Ok Google* detection to prevent the baby (or the doorbell) accidentally giving commands.

Given these restrictions, and the fact that you won't be able to use your phone while it's listening for the baby or the doorbell, you may be better off either listening for cries or chimes yourself, either directly or using conventional monitoring electronics.

- **Flash Notification.** Tap this button to display the Flash Notification screen. You can then set the Camera Light switch to On to make your phone flash the camera light when notifications arrive or when alarms ring. You can also set the Screen switch to On to have the phone flash the screen instead. Lay the phone screen down so that you can see the flash when it triggers. Turn the phone over to stop the flashing.
- **Mute All Sounds.** Set this switch to On if you want to disable all sound, including that from the speakerphone.
- **Samsung Subtitles.** Tap this button to display the Samsung Subtitles (CC) screen. Here, you can set the switch at the top to On or Off to control whether apps on your phone that support Samsung Subtitles, such as the Video app, display those subtitles. If you set the switch to On, you can also choose the style, alignment, font, and text size for the subtitles. Once you've made your choices, you can turn Samsung Subtitles on or off quickly by setting the Samsung Subtitles (CC)

switch on the Hearing screen.

Note: The "CC" on the Samsung Subtitles screen and the Google Subtitles screen stands for closed captioning.

- **Google Subtitles.** Tap this button to display the Google Subtitles (CC) screen. Here, you can set the switch at the top to On or Off to control whether apps on your phone that support Google Subtitles display those subtitles. If you set the switch to On, you can also choose the language, text size, and caption size for the subtitles. Once you've made your choices, you can turn Google Subtitles on or off quickly by setting the Google Subtitles (CC) switch on the Hearing screen.
- **Left/Right Sound Balance.** Drag this slider to adjust the sound balance between the left and right sides of connected headphones or earphones. The slider is available only when you've connected headphones or earphones to your Galaxy S8.
- **Mono Audio.** Set this switch to On if you want to play mono audio through a single earphone.

Choose Dexterity and Interaction Options

The Dexterity and Interaction options contain numerous settings that are designed to make it easier for users to interact with their phone according to each users' specific habits.

Follow these steps to access the Dexterity and Interaction options screen:

1. Open the *Settings* app. For example, swipe up or down on the *Home* screen, and then tap the **Settings** icon on the *Apps* screen.
2. Tap the **Accessibility** button toward the bottom of the *Settings* screen.
3. Tap the **Dexterity and Interaction** button in the *Categories* list at the top of the *Accessibility* screen.
4. The *Dexterity and Interaction* screen is displayed as shown:

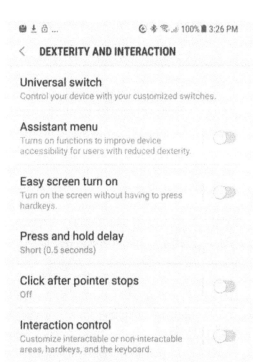

The following sections introduce you to the options you can set on the Dexterity and Interaction screen.

Universal Switch

Tapping the **Universal Switch** button displays the *Universal Switch* screen, which enables you to configure customizable switches to help you communicate with your phone.

Note: The "switches" used for Universal Switch can be physical accessories that you connect to your phone, but you can also use the screen and the phone's camera as switches. For example, you can set the camera to detect movement of your head, eyes, and mouth.

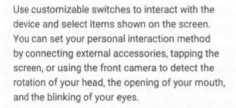

< UNIVERSAL SWITCH   SETTINGS

OFF

Use customizable switches to interact with the
device and select items shown on the screen.
You can set your personal interaction method
by connecting external accessories, tapping the
screen, or using the front camera to detect the
rotation of your head, the opening of your mouth,
and the blinking of your eyes.

To get started, try to move the switch at the top to *On*; the switch doesn't move unless you've set up a switch, but it displays a dialog box in which you can tap the **Add Switch** button to start adding a switch.

Assistant Menu

Tap this button to display the Assistant Menu screen, and then set the switch at the top to On to display the Assistant Menu icon, the gray circle containing four rounded rectangles that you can see on the

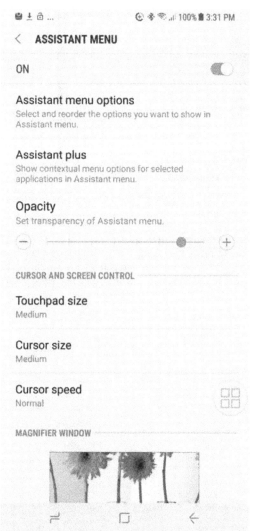

right of the Cursor Speed button.

Once you've displayed the Assistant Menu icon, you can tap the icon to display the Assistant Menu at any point. The Assistant Menu is straightforward to use:

- **Screen Number.** The Assistant Menu has multiple screens. The readout, such as 1/4, shows which screen of the Assistant Menu you're viewing.
- **Previous Screen.** Tap the < button to display the previous screen.
- **Next Screen.** Tap the > button to display the next screen.
- **Open an Item.** Tap the item you want to open.

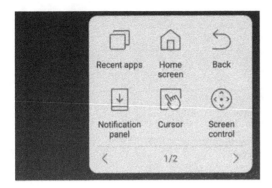

The remaining controls on the Assistant Menu screen enable you to configure the Assistant Menu to suit the way you use your phone:

- **Assistant Menu Options.** Tap this button to display the Assistant Menu Options screen, which enables you to rearrange the menu. Tap the white circle containing a red minus sign (-) to remove an item; tap a white circle with a green plus sign (+) at the bottom of the screen to add that item. Tap the ← button or the Back button when you finish editing the Assistant Menu.

- **Assistant Plus.** This feature enables you to use extra features in the Assistant Menu in the apps you specify. Tap this button to display the Assistant Plus screen. Here, you can set the switch at the top to On to enable the Assistant Plus feature, and then set the switch to On for each app you want to use. Once you've made your choices, you can turn Assistant Plus on or off quickly by setting the Assistant Plus switch on the Assistant Menu screen.

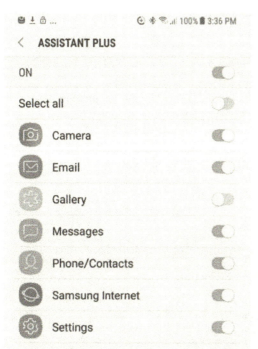

- **Touchpad Size.** Tap this button to display the pop-up menu, and then tap the Small item, the Medium item, or the Large item to control the size of the touchpad that appears when you turn on the Cursor feature in Assistant Menu.
- **Cursor Size.** Tap this button to display the pop-up menu, and then tap the Medium item or the Large item to control the size of the cursor that appears when you turn on the Cursor feature.
- **Cursor Speed.** Tap this button to display the pop-up menu, and then tap the Slow item, the Normal item, or the Fast item to control the movement speed of the cursor that appears when you turn on the Cursor feature.
- **Zoom Percentage.** Drag this slider to set the zoom percentage for the Magnifier Window feature.
- **Magnifier Size.** Tap this pop-up menu and then tap the Small item, the Medium item, or the Large item to control the size of the Magnifier Window.

Easy Screen Turn On

If you want to be able to turn the screen on your phone back on easily after it goes off, set the Easy Screen Turn On switch to On. You can then swipe your hand above the screen from left to right to turn the screen back on. If you want to see an illustration of the gesture, tap the main part of the Easy Screen Turn On button to display the Easy Screen Turn On screen.

Tip: The *Easy Screen Turn on* feature can be handy if your hands are too dirty to touch your phone but not actually dripping anything offensive—for example, when you're cooking and have the recipe displayed on screen.

Press and Hold Delay

Press and hold delay can adjust the amount of time it takes for a touch to be registered as a "click" on the Galaxy S8 device. This can be useful when configuring a phone for use by an individual with physical disabilities, among others.

*Follow these steps to configure the length of time it takes for your phone to register a press-and-hold touch:*Open the *Settings* app. For example, swipe up or down on the *Home* screen, and then tap the **Settings** icon on the *Apps* screen.Tap the **Accessibility** button toward the bottom of the *Settings* screen.

1. Open the *Settings* app. For example, swipe up or down on the *Home* screen, and then tap the **Settings** icon on the *Apps* screen.
2. Tap the **Accessibility** button toward the bottom of the *Settings* screen.
3. Tap the **Dexterity and Interaction** button in the *Categories* list at the top of the *Accessibility* screen.
4. Tap the **Press and Hold Delay** button.
5. Tap the appropriate option button in the *Press and Hold Delay* dialog box as shown:

- **Short (0.5 Seconds).** This is the default setting.
- **Medium (1.0 Second).**
- **Long (1.5 Seconds).**
- **Custom.** If you tap this option button, the Press and Hold Delay screen appears. Tap and hold the large blue button for the length of time you want to use, and then tap the Save button.

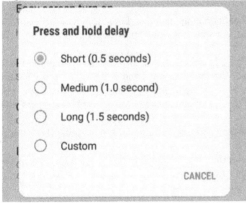

Click After Pointer Stops

If, when you connect a mouse or trackpad, you want the Galaxy S8 to automatically click an object on which the pointer stops moving, set the *Click After Pointer* switch to *On*. If you need to configure the delay between the movement stopping and the click occurring, tap the main part of the **Click After Pointer Stops** button, and then drag the *Delay Before Click* slider on the *Click After Pointer Steps* screen.

Follow these steps to adjust the Click After Pointer Stops settings:

Interaction Control

The Interaction Control feature enables you to block certain areas of the screen from registering touches—for example, if you find you touch the screen unintentionally.

Follow these steps to configure interaction control:

1. Tap the***Interaction Control*** button on the *Dexterity and Interaction* screen to display the *Interaction Control* screen.
2. Here, set the switch at the top to *On* if you want to enable the feature, and then read the explanatory text below the diagram.
3. Set the *Use Screen Lock When Turned Off* switch to *On* if you want the Galaxy S8 to lock the screen when it is turned off.

11

Configure the Edge Screen Features

The Edge screen on the Galaxy S8 gives you quick access to information. This chapter explains how to use the Edge screen, which include the following features:

- **Edge Panels.** You can choose which information panels to display on the Edge screens. For example, you might want to display the *People Edge* panel (which helps you stay in touch with your contacts), the *Apps Edge* panel (which lets you launch your favorite apps quickly), and the *Tasks Edge* panel (which provides shortcuts to tasks, contacts, alarms and timers, and more).
- **Edge Lighting.** You can configure the Edge screen to light up when you receive calls and notifications. You can set different colors for different contacts, so you can tell by the color who is calling you.
- **Quick Reply.** You can reject an incoming call from one of your My People and automatically send the caller a canned message by placing your finger on the heart-rate sensor for two seconds.
- **Edge Feeds.** You can set the Edge screen to display your Edge Feeds, which are customizable tickers of information. For example, you can display information about missed calls or incoming messages on the Edge screen.

Configure the Edge Screen Features

The *Edge* screen can be configured by using the *Edge* screen in the *Settings* app.

Follow these steps to configure the Edge screen features:

1. Open the *Settings* app.
2. Tap the **Display** button to show the *Display* screen.

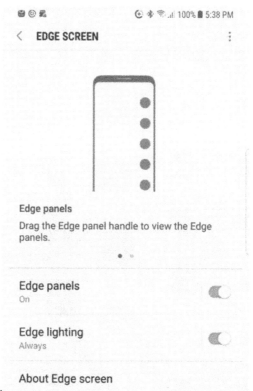

Edge panels

Drag the Edge panel handle to view the Edge panels.

Edge panels
On

Edge lighting
Always

About Edge screen

3. Tap the **Edge Screen** button.

You can swipe left on the preview at the top of the screen to display more information about the Edge screen. The the Edge Panels button and the Edge Lighting in the lower half of the screen enable you to configure the Edge Screen features, as explained in the rest of this section. The switch at the right side of each button enables you to turn on or off each of these features quickly from the Edge Screen screen rather than having to go to the individual screens.

Choose Which Edge Panels to Use and Their Order

The Galaxy S8 comes with a selection of Edge panels that you can display on the Edge screen. You can enable and disable panels as needed, and you can control the order for the panels you choose to display. You can also choose whether to display the Edge screen content on the Edge screen on the right of the Galaxy S8 or on the Edge screen on the left. The right Edge screen is the default. You make this choice from the Handle Settings screen, which you access from the Edge Panels screen.

Choose Your Edge Panels

To choose your Edge panels, follow these steps:

1. Tap the **Edge Panels** button on the *Edge Screen* screen to display the *Edge Panels* screen.

2. Set the switch at the top of the *Edge Panels* screen to *On* to enable Edge panels.
3. Check the check circle for each Edge panel you want to use. Swipe left on the list of Edge panels to display other panels that are available.

If an Edge panel whose check box you check has an Edit button at its bottom, as the Apps Edge panel and the People Edge panel do, you can tap the Edit button to display the screen for editing that panel's contents. See the following sections for details on editing the default Edge panels.

Configure the Apps Edge Panel

If you choose to display the Apps Edge panel, you should configure it to make it show the apps you want.

Follow these steps to configure which apps are displayed on the Apps Edge panel:

1. Tap the **Edit** button below the *Apps Edge* panel to display the *Apps Edge* screen as shown below.

HOME SCREEN SHORTCUTS

Shortcuts you create on the
Home screen from within a
specific app will also appear
here.

CALENDAR

Create
event/task

Search for
event/task

CAMERA

Take
selfie

Take pics
(Auto)

CLOCK

Add alarm

World clock

Stopwatch

Timer

CONTACTS

Compose
message

Take
selfie

View
bookmarks

Create
event/task

Create
contact

Add alarm

Snap
window

Take
screenshots

2. Edit and rearrange the apps as explained in the following list:

- **Add an app to the Apps Edge panel.** Tap the app in either the *Frequently Used Apps* list or the *All Apps* list (the list below the Frequently Used Apps list) on the left side of the screen.
- **Remove an app from the Apps Edge panel.** Tap the red minus (-) sign on the upper-right corner of the app's icon on the right side of the screen.
- **Rearrange the icons on the Apps Edge panel.** Tap an icon on the right side of the screen and drag it to the icon with which you want to swap it. Drop the icon, and the icons exchange places.

3. Tap the< button in the upper-left corner of the screen or the *Back* button below the screen to return to the *Edge Panels* screen.

Configure the People Edge Panel

If you choose to display the People Edge panel, configure it to display the five contacts whose communications you most want to receive. You can also enable or disable the OnCircle app, which enables you to send pictures, stickers, and other graphical messages to these contacts, provided that they too register for OnCircle.

To configure the People Edge panel, follow these steps:

1. Tap the **Edit** button on the *People Edge* panel to display the *People Edge* screen. At first, this screen is empty, but the left pane provides a Suggestions list of frequent contacts and a **Select**

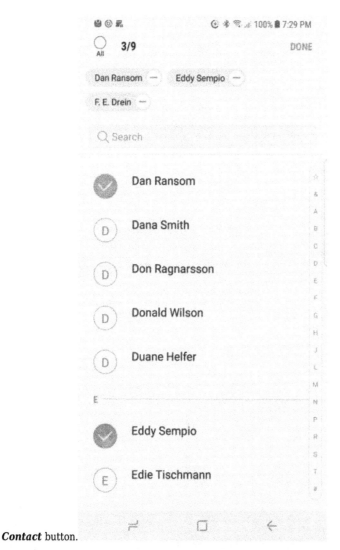

Contact button.

Note: If your phone prompts you to allow People Edge to make and manage phone calls, and to send and view SMS messages, tap the **Allow** button in each dialog box.

2. If you want to add one or more contacts from the Suggestions list to *People Edge*, tap the appropriate buttons in the Suggestions list.

3. To add other contacts, tap the **Select Contact** button. On the *Select Contacts* screen that appears, tap each contact in turn, adding them to the list at the top of the screen. A readout such as 2/9 appears at the top of the screen, showing that you have added two contacts out of the nine possible. Tap the **Done** button when you finish.

4. Edit and rearrange the contacts as explained in the following list:

- **Remove a contact.** Tap the red minus (–) icon on the contact's icon. The contact disappears from the list, and an Add Contact button appears instead.
- **Add a contact.** Tap an Select Contact button to display the Contacts screen, tap the contact, and then tap the Add button.
- **Change the order of contacts.** Tap the up-and-down arrow button on a contact and drag the contact up or down the list.

Note: You can lock the People Edge panel while your phone is securely locked. To do so, tap the *Advanced* button to display the *Advanced* screen, and then set the *Hide Content on Lock Screen* switch to *On*.

5. Tap the **<** button in the upper-left corner of the screen or the **Back** button below the screen to return to the main *People Edge* screen.

Configure the Tasks Edge Panel

The Tasks Edge panel lets you quickly take task-related actions, such as creating an event in the Calendar app, creating a contact in the Contacts app, composing a new instant message, or taking a selfie.

To configure the Tasks Edge panel, follow these steps from the Edge Panels screen:

1. Tap the **Edit** icon on the *Tasks Edge* panel to display the *Tasks Edge* screen.

2. Edit and rearrange the task shortcuts as explained in the following list:

- **Add a task shortcut.** Tap the task shortcut in the left column. Scroll down to see the full list of task shortcuts available.
- **Remove a task shortcut.** Tap the red minus (-) icon on the task's icon in the right column. The task icon disappears from the list.
- **Rearrange your task shortcuts.** Tap a task shortcut in the right pane and drag it to where you want it to appear.

3. Tap the < button in the upper-left corner of the screen or the **Back** button below the screen to return to the *Edge Panels* screen.

Download Other Edge Panels

The Galaxy S8 comes with plenty of Edge panels to get you started. But if you find the Edge screen useful, you might want to explore other Edge panels that are available. There is an impressively wide variety of Edge panels.

To see which Edge panels are available, tap the **Download** button at the top of the Edge Panels screen. Your phone launches or activates the *Galaxy Apps* app, which displays the selection of Edge panels available. You can tap the *All* tab, the *Paid* tab, the *Free* tab, or the *New* tab at the top of the screen, and then browse the Edge panels that appear; or tap the **Search** button in the upper-right corner of the screen and type search terms for what you want to find.

Change the Order of Your Edge Panels

Once you've chosen the Edge panels you want to display, and configured their contents as needed, move the Edge panels into your preferred order.

Follow these steps to rearrange edge panels:

1. Tap the **Menu** button (the three vertical dots) on the *Edge Panels* screen, and then tap the **Reorder** item on the menu.
2. The *Reorder* screen appears as shown below. Tap the **< >** symbol at the top of an Edge panel and

Drag one of the < > icons to the left or right to reorder your Edge panels.

drag it left or right to where you want it.

3. Once you've gotten the Edge panels into the order you want, tap the< button in the upper-left corner of the screen or the **Back** button below the screen to return to the *Edge Panels* screen.

Configure Edge Panel Position and Handle Settings

Next, spend a few minutes configuring the Edge panel position and the settings for the Edge panel handle. The Edge panel handle is the tab-like line at the side of the screen that indicates where you can pull to open the Edge panel.

To customize the Edge panel position and Edge panel handle, follow these steps:

1. On the *Edge Panels* screen, tap the **Menu** button (the three vertical dots) and then tap the**Handle Settings** item on the menu to display the *Edge Panel Handle Settings* screen.

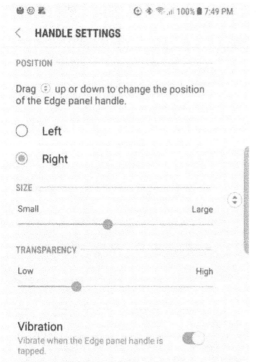

POSITION

Drag up or down to change the position of the Edge panel handle.

○ Left

⦿ Right

SIZE

Small   Large

TRANSPARENCY

Low   High

Vibration
Vibrate when the Edge panel handle is tapped.

2. Tap the **up-and-down arrow handle** next to the blue Edge handle on the current Edge side of the screen (the right side in the example) and drag the Edge handle to where you want it.

3. To change the side of the screen on which the Edge panel handle appears, tap the **Left option** button or the **Right option** button, as needed.

4. To change the size of the Edge panel handle, drag the **Size** slider along the *Small–Large* axis.

5. To adjust the transparency of the Edge panel handle, drag the **Transparency** slider along the *Low–High* axis.

6. Set the **Vibration** switch to *On* if you want your phone to vibrate when you tap the Edge handle.

7. Tap the < button in the upper-left corner of the screen or the **Back** button below the screen to return to the *Edge Panels* screen.

8. From the *Edge Panels* screen, tap the < button in the upper-left corner of the screen or the **Back** button below the screen to display the *Edge Screen* screen again.

Configure the Edge Lighting Feature and the Quick Reply Feature

The Galaxy S8 Edge enables you to configure the Edge screen to light up when you receive calls and notifications. You can also enable or disable the Quick Reply feature, which lets you send a quick response to a caller by placing your finger on the heart rate sensor on the back of the phone for a couple of seconds when it rings in a screen-down position. There's only one Quick Reply message, but you can edit it ahead of time to make it say what you need it to say.

To configure the Edge Lighting feature and the Quick Reply feature, follow these steps:

1. Tap the **Edge Lighting** button on the *Edge Screen* screen to display the *Edge Lighting* screen.

2. Set the switch at the top of the screen to *On* if you want to use the *Edge Lighting* feature.
3. In the *Show Edge Lighting* section, select the **When Screen Is On** option button, the **When Screen Is Off** option button, or the **Always** option button, as appropriate.
4. Tap the **Manage Notifications** button to display the *Manage Notifications* screen.

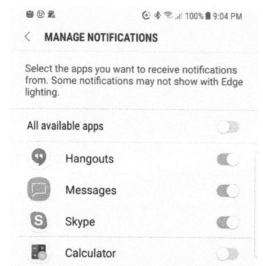

Select the apps you want to receive notifications from. Some notifications may not show with Edge lighting.

All available apps

Hangouts

Messages

Skype

Calculator

5. Set the switch to *On* for each app from which you want to receive notifications on the Edge panel. You can set the All Available Apps switch at the top of the list to On if you want Edge notifications for all the apps that can produce them, but usually it's more effective to choose only the apps you'll find most helpful.

6. Tap the < button in the upper-left corner of the screen or the **Back** button below the screen to return to the *Edge Lighting* screen.

7. Tap the **Menu** button (the three vertical dots) to open the menu, and then tap the **Quick Reply** item. The *Quick Reply* screen opens.

When the screen is off and the phone is turned face down, incoming calls will show on Edge lighting. Decline an incoming call and send a preset message to the caller by placing your finger on the heart rate sensor for 2 seconds.

QUICK REPLY MESSAGE

Sorry, I can't talk right now. I'll call you back.

8. Set the switch at the top to *On* if you want to use the *Quick Reply* feature.
9. In the *Quick Reply Message* area, tap to place the insertion point, and then edit the text to make it read the way you want.
10. Tap the< button in the upper-left corner of the screen or the **Back** button below the screen to return to the *Edge Lighting* screen.
11. Tap the< button in the upper-left corner of the screen or the **Back** button below the screen to return to the *Edge Screen* screen.

12

Use the Edge Screen Features

Once the Edge screen features are configured to work the way you prefer, you can make the most of the features by using *Edge panels.* The Edge screen can be adjusted in infinite ways that are designed to make it easier for you to interact with your phone. Edge panels can be configured so that your most often used features and apps are at your fingertips.

Open the Edge Screen

Follow these steps to make use of the Edge screen:

1. Open the *Edge* screen, by dragging the *Edge handle* from its side toward the center of the screen.

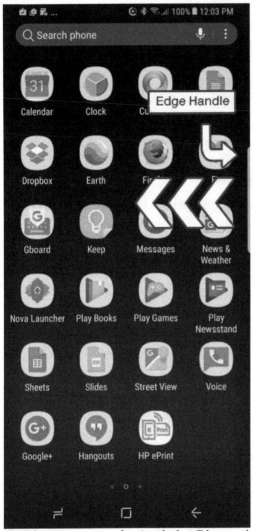

2. The *Edge* screen opens, showing the last Edge panel used.

The line of white dots in the lower-left corner of the screen shows the number of *Edge* panels available, with the larger white dot representing the current panel.

Change the Edge Panel Displayed

Perform this step to change the Edge panel displayed:

1. Swipe left or right on the current panel. The next Edge panel in that direction appears.

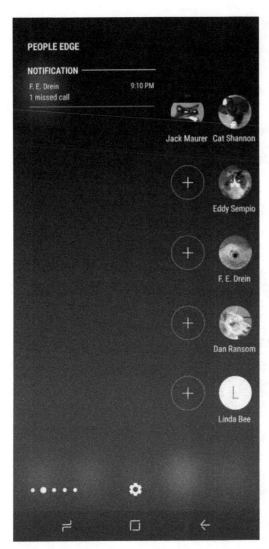

Note: Alternatively, tap one of the white dots in the lower-left corner of the screen. Tapping a dot is a faster way to make large jumps if you use many Edge panels, but you need to tap precisely.

Take Actions with the Edge Panels

Once you've displayed the Edge panel you need, you can quickly take actions with it. Here are three quick examples:

- **Apps Edge panel.** Tap the app you want to open.
- **People Edge panel.** Tap a notification summary to display the event that raised the

notification—for instance, tap a message notification to display the conversation in the Messages app. Tap a contact name to display options for contacting that person.

- **Tasks Edge panel.** Tap the icon for the action you want to take, such as *Compose Message* or *Create Contact*. The appropriate app becomes active, and you can complete the action.

Tip: You can tap the Settings icon (the gear icon) at the bottom of any Edge panel to display the Edge Panels screen in the Settings app.

Reject a Call and Send a Quick Reply

When one of your My People contacts calls, and you don't want to take the call, place your finger on the heart-rate sensor for two seconds. Your Galaxy S8 Edge sends the call to voicemail and automatically texts your Quick Reply message to the caller.

13

Secure Your Galaxy S8 Against Local Threats

Thanks to its wide array of features, your Galaxy S8 likely contains a huge amount of personal data and valuable information. You should strongly consider securing that information against both local threats, such as the wrong people picking up the phone and using it, and Internet threats, such as people stealing your data across the Internet.

Understand Your Options for Securing Your Galaxy S8

- **Unlock method.** Choose an unlock method to prevent unauthorized access to your phone.
- **Lock your phone quickly.** You can control how quickly your phone locks.
- **Enable the Auto Factory Reset feature.** You can set your phone to automatically wipe its data if someone tries and fails to unlock the phone 15 times in a row.
- **Set up Smart Lock.** The Smart Lock feature lets you choose to prevent your phone from locking automatically under other conditions. There's also a way of unlocking your phone using your voice.
- **Set your owner information.** You can display information on the lock screen to help anyone who finds your phone to return it to you.
- **Enable the Find My Mobile feature.** The Find My Mobile feature enables you to locate your phone, if it goes missing, by using your Samsung account.
- **Disallow apps from unknown sources.** You can prevent the installation of apps from sources other than the Play Store and the Galaxy Apps Store.
- **Enable the Secure Startup feature.** Secure Startup requires you to enter your PIN when starting Android (way before the lock screen).
- **Choose other security settings.** Beyond the security features and settings explained so far in this list, your phone offers others, such as choosing whether to make passwords visible and installing and using security certificates.
- **Encrypt the contents of the SD card.** Android version 7 (Nougat) encrypts the contents of the phone's internal storage automatically, and Samsung doesn't give you a way to remove the encryption. You can encrypt the contents of the SD card as well, as explained in the section "Encrypt the SD Card" in Chapter 9.
- **Use the Secure Folder feature.** The Galaxy S8 includes a feature called Secure Folder that enables you to put important or sensitive files into a secure container to protect them against prying eyes.

Secure Your Galaxy S8 with the Right Unlock Method

When you start the Galaxy S8, it normally displays the lock screen. The lock screen is a security barrier to prevent unauthorized people from using the phone.

You can choose among seven means of unlocking the lock screen:

- **Swipe.** This is the weakest form of unlocking: You unlock the Galaxy S8 by swiping your finger across the screen. This provides no security—all it does is make sure that the phone doesn't get unlocked in your bag or in your pocket.

Caution: You can't use the Swipe unlock method if you use certain other security-related features, such as virtual private networking. If you try to use any such feature, Android walks you through the process of applying an effective screen lock before allowing you to use the feature.

- **Pattern.** This form of unlocking uses a grid of nine dots on which you draw a pattern with your finger. Pattern unlock can be good for children, but it provides only moderate security, so you probably won't want to use it for your own account. Pattern requires a PIN as a backup way of unlocking.
- **PIN.** PIN unlock requires you to enter a Personal Identification Number (PIN) of four or more digits to unlock the device. A PIN provides reasonable security, especially if you use eight or more digits, but a password is better.
- **Password.** Password unlock requires you to enter a password of four or more characters to unlock the Galaxy S8. By using a longer password (such as 10 characters or more) and by mixing uppercase and lowercase letters with numbers and symbols, you can secure your phone pretty tightly.
- **Face.** Face unlock requires you to lift the Galaxy S8 and point it at your face, which preferably isn't obscured by glasses, excessive facial hair, or excessive makeup.

Note: You can't use both Face unlock and Iris unlock at the same time—the Galaxy S8 can manage one or the other, but not both at once. Samsung warns users that Face unlock is not very secure (especially if you have a twin), so if you're deciding between Face and Iris, choose Iris over Face.

- **Fingerprints.** You can scan one or more of your fingerprints and then use unlock your phone by placing one of those fingers (or thumbs) on the fingerprint scanner on the back of the Galaxy S8 . Fingerprints provide pretty strong security but require a PIN or a password as a backup unlock method.
- **Irises.** You can scan your irises and then unlock your phone by gazing at the camera at the top of your phone's screen. As of this writing, the security level of iris scanning is not entirely clear, although it seems to be significantly better than Face unlock. Iris scanning requires a PIN or a password as a backup unlock method.

For effective security, you really need to use fingerprint unlock, PIN unlock, or Password unlock.

Caution: Fingerprint unlock is usually the most convenient way of unlocking your phone; iris unlock can also be convenient. But there's a legal wrinkle you should be aware of, at least in the United States: Law enforcement may be able to compel you to unlock your phone using your fingerprint without a search warrant, whereas it cannot compel you to provide a password or passcode. This is because the fingerprint is considered "real or physical evidence" whereas a password or passcode is considered "communication." It seems likely that iris scanning will also be considered "real or physical evidence." As of this writing, these distinctions are still being argued in courts; so if you will rely on them, you would be wise to search online to learn the current state of affairs.

Start Setting Your Unlock Method

Here's how to start setting your unlock method:

1. Open the *Settings* app. For example, tap the **Settings** icon on the *Apps* screen.

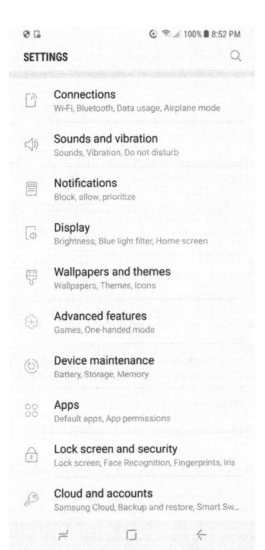

SETTINGS   Q

Connections
Wi-Fi, Bluetooth, Data usage, Airplane mode

Sounds and vibration
Sounds, Vibration, Do not disturb

Notifications
Block, allow, prioritize

Display
Brightness, Blue light filter, Home screen

Wallpapers and themes
Wallpapers, Themes, Icons

Advanced features
Games, One-handed mode

Device maintenance
Battery, Storage, Memory

Apps
Default apps, App permissions

Lock screen and security
Lock screen, Face Recognition, Fingerprints, Iris

Cloud and accounts
Samsung Cloud, Backup and restore, Smart Sw...

2. Tap the *Lock Screen and Security* button to display the *Lock Screen and Security* screen.

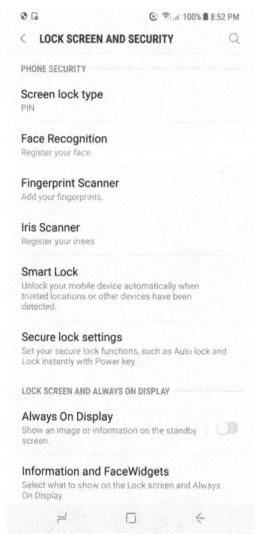

PHONE SECURITY

Screen lock type
PIN

Face Recognition
Register your face.

Fingerprint Scanner
Add your fingerprints.

Iris Scanner
Register your irises.

Smart Lock
Unlock your mobile device automatically when
trusted locations or other devices have been
detected.

Secure lock settings
Set your secure lock functions, such as Auto lock and
Lock instantly with Power key.

LOCK SCREEN AND ALWAYS ON DISPLAY

Always On Display
Show an image or information on the standby
screen.

Information and FaceWidgets
Select what to show on the Lock screen and Always
On Display.

3. Tap the *Screen Lock Type* button. If you're currently using any unlock method except Swipe, you'll need to enter your PIN or passcode to authenticate yourself. The *Screen Lock Type* screen

4. Tap the button for the means of unlocking you want to use, and then proceed as explained in the following subsections.

Set the Pattern Unlock Method

Follow these steps to set the Pattern unlock method:

1. Navigate to the *Set PIN* screen by selecting **Settings > Lock screen and security > screen lock type > Pattern** as described above.
2. To set the Pattern unlock method, simply draw your pattern on the *Pattern* screen, and then tap

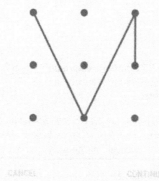

Release finger when finished.

Remember this Pattern. It will be required after restarting the device.

the **Continue** button.

3. Android prompts you to draw the pattern again to confirm it. Do so, and then tap the **Confirm** button to set the pattern.

4. The *Notifications on Lock Screen* screen then appears, and you can choose which notifications to display on the lock screen.

Set the PIN Unlock Method

Follow these steps to set the PIN unlock method:

1. Navigate to the *Set PIN* screen by selecting **Settings > Lock screen and security > screen**

lock type > PIN as described earlier.

2. The Continue button is unavailable until you type at least four digits, which is the minimum length for the PIN. Enter at least 4 digits and tap the **Continue** button.

SET PIN

PIN must contain at least 4 digits.

•••

Remember this PIN. It will be required after restarting
the device.

CANCEL   CONTINUE

3. When you tap the **Continue** button, Android prompts you to enter the PIN again to confirm it. Re-enter the PIN exactly as entered the previous time.
4. Press the **OK** button to confirm.

Once these steps are complete, the PIN is set. The *Notifications on Lock Screen* screen then appears, and you can choose which notifications to display on the lock screen, which is an important feature for many users. These notifications are displayed on the lock screen, above the unlock field.

Set the Password Unlock Method

Follow these steps to set the password unlock method:

1. Navigate to the *Set PIN* screen by selecting **Settings > Lock screen and security > screen lock type > Password** as described earlier.
2. Type the password you want to use on the *Set Password* screen. The password must be at least four characters long and contain at least one letter, but to get effective security you should use at least 8-12 characters with a mixture of letters (in both uppercase and lowercase), numbers, and

SET PASSWORD

Tap Continue when finished.

••••••••

Remember this Password. It will be required after
restarting the device.

CANCEL   CONTINUE

symbols.

3. After typing your password, tap the **Continue** button. Type the password again on the
   confirmation screen, and then tap the **OK** button. Android sets the password. The *Notifications on
   Lock Screen* screen then appears, and you can choose which notifications to display on the lock
   screen.

Set the Face Unlock Method

Follow these steps to set the face unlock method:

1. Navigate to the *Face Setting* screen by selecting **Settings > Lock screen and security >
   screen lock type > Face** as described earlier.
2. Set the Face slider in the *Biometrics* section of the *Screen Lock Type* screen to *On*. An instruction
   screen appears, telling you to hold the phone in front of your face.

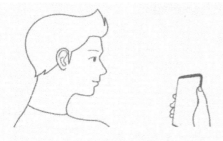

Get ready to unlock your phone by showing your face.

For best results, set up face recognition indoors or away from direct sunlight.

3. Hold the phone as shown, and tap the **Continue** button.
4. On the screen that appears, move the phone (or your head) to position your head within the circle. After a moment, a message appears saying that your face has been recognized.
5. The *Faster Recognition* screen then appears. Set the switch at the top of the screen to *On* if you want to use faster recognition, which recognizes faces more quickly but may be less accurate than

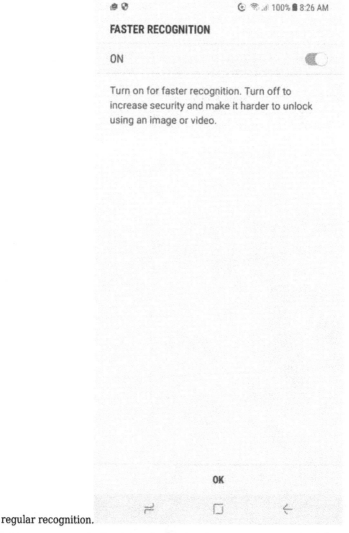

FASTER RECOGNITION

ON

Turn on for faster recognition. Turn off to
increase security and make it harder to unlock
using an image or video.

OK

regular recognition.

Caution: Enabling Faster Recognition increases the possibility of Face Unlock being fooled by a photo
or video of you.

6. After making your choice, tap the **OK** button at the bottom of the *Faster Recognition* screen. The
Lock Screen and Security screen then appears again.

Set Up the Fingerprints Unlock Method

If you use your phone extensively, you'll likely find fingerprints to be the most convenient unlock
method because it's quick and you can do it without looking at the screen.

Tip: It's a good idea to register multiple fingerprints so that you can unlock your phone with either hand. Another advantage is that you'll still be able to unlock your phone if you damage the skin on one of your fingertips. You can add up to four fingerprints.

When you set the Fingerprints switch on the *Lock Screen and Security* screen to *On,* and then enter your current PIN, password, or pattern, the *Scan Your Fingerprint* screen appears.

Follow these steps to set the fingerprint unlock method:

1. Navigate to the *Set Fingerprint* screen by selecting **Settings > Lock screen and security > screen lock type > Fingerprint** as described earlier.

Scan your fingerprint

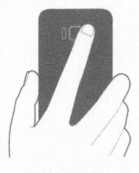

Place a finger on the fingerprint sensor, lift it off,
then repeat. Move your finger left or right slightly
between attempts.

2. Place your finger on the sensor on the back of the phone, and then follow the prompts to scan it.

Scan your fingerprint

70%

Place your finger on the fingerprint sensor, then
lift it off again.

3. When you finish adding your fingerprint, the *Fingerprint Added* screen appears.

Fingerprint added

Add another fingerprint?

ADD   DONE

⇄   ☐   ←

4. Tap the **Add** button if you want to add another fingerprint. Otherwise, tap the **Done** button to the *Lock Screen and Security* screen.

Managing Fingerprints

Now that you've added one or more fingerprints, you can rename the fingerprints and tell your phone how to use them.

Follow these steps to rename and manage fingerprints:

1. Tap the **Fingerprint Scanner** button on the *Lock Screen and Security* screen to display the *Fingerprint Scanner* screen; you'll need to provide your PIN, pattern, or password to get there.

2. From here, you can take the following actions:

- **Rename the fingerprint.** Tap the Fingerprint 1 button to display the Rename Fingerprint dialog box; type a descriptive name, such as Right Index Finger; and then tap the Rename button.

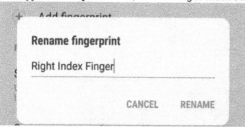

- **Add another fingerprint.** Tap the Add Fingerprint button and follow through the process of registering it.
- **Samsung Pass.** If you want to use your fingerprint as a quick way to sign in to websites, tap the Samsung Pass button. View the information on the screens that appear, and then tap the Start button and sign in to your Samsung account. If your phone prompts you to update Samsung Pass, tap the Update button to install the update.
- **Samsung Account.** Set the Samsung Account switch to On if you want to use your fingerprint to authenticate you to Samsung services. You'll need to type your account password.
- **Fingerprint Unlock.** Set the Fingerprint Unlock switch to On if you want to use your fingerprint to unlock your phone. Normally you'll want to do this.

- **Remove a fingerprint.** Tap the Edit button at the top of the Fingerprints screen to display the Select Fingerprints screen. Tap the check box for each fingerprint you want to remove, and then

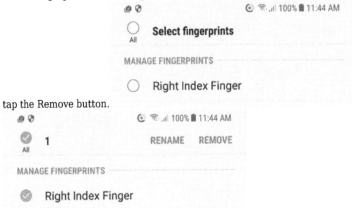

tap the Remove button.

Set Up the Irises Unlock Method

Follow these steps to set the iris unlock method:

1. Navigate to the *Set Iris* screen by selecting **Settings > Lock screen and security > screen lock type > Iris** as described earlier.
2. If the slider next to *Iris* is *Off*, set it to *On*.
3. If Face Unlock is enabled, the Use Iris Unlock? dialog box will open instead, telling you that you can't use both Iris Unlock and Face Unlock at the same time, and that Face Unlock will be turned

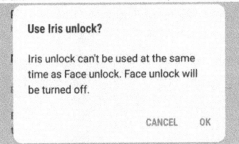

off. Tap the **OK** button.
4. A huge disclaimer dialog then opens. Read all the warnings and caveats, and then tap the **OK** button if you want to proceed.

Note: For iris recognition to work well, Samsung recommends you remove your glasses or contact lenses. Removing your glasses to unlock your phone may be acceptable for some people, but for most people, removing contact lenses makes iris recognition absurdly impractical.

5. The instructions screen for registering your irises then appears. Tap the **Continue** button when you're ready to proceed.
6. Follow the instructions for positioning your eyes in the circles on the screen so that the phone can capture your irises, and then read through the several screens of instructions that follow. The

Lock Screen and Security screen then appears again.

7. To configure what you can do with Iris Unlock, tap the **Iris Scanner** button, and then enter your PIN, pattern, or password to get to the *Iris Scanner* screen as shown.

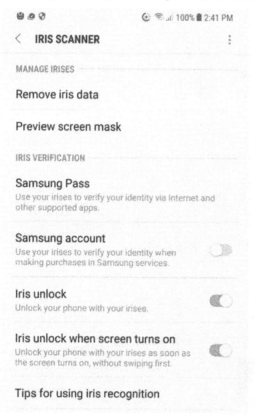

From the Iris Scanner screen, you can take the following actions:

- **Remove your iris data.** Tap the Remove button at the top of the screen.
- **Apply a mask to the preview screen.** Tap the Preview Screen Mask button to display the Preview Screen Mask screen. Tap the mask you want to use, and then tap the < button in the upper-left corner of the screen or the Back button below the screen.

- **Enable Samsung Pass.** If you want to use your irises to sign in to websites, tap the **Samsung Pass** button. On the screens that appear, read the information, and then tap the **Start** button and sign in to your Samsung account.
- **Authenticate to your Samsung Account.** Set the *Samsung Account* switch to *On* if you want to use your irises to authenticate you to Samsung services.
- **Enable or disable Iris Unlock.** Set the *Iris Unlock* switch to *On* if you want to use your irises to unlock your phone.
- **Enable or disable Iris Unlock When Screen Turns On.** Set the *Iris Unlock When Screen Turns On* switch to *On* if you want to be able to unlock your phone via your irises without having to swipe. Normally, you'll want to enable this feature.

- **View tips on using iris recognition.** Tap the ***Tips on Using Iris Recognition*** button if you want to look through the tips on using iris recognition again: hold the phone at eye level, remove your glasses or contacts, and so on.

8. Make the selection that you would like and continue setup if necessary, or exit from *Settings* app entirely to cancel any changes made.

14

Set Up Any Smart Lock Methods Needed

As well as the unlock methods explained in the previous section, Android includes a feature called Smart Lock that gives you three ways to keep your phone unlocked under certain conditions and one way to unlock it quickly.

Caution: Think carefully before enabling Smart Lock. It's an appealing feature and can make your phone easier to use. But because neither any of the smart stay-unlocked methods nor the smart unlock method is foolproof, using Smart Lock can compromise the security of your device. You may be better off not using Smart Lock and using your fingerprints or your irises to unlock your device quickly.

These are the three Smart Lock methods for keeping your phone unlocked:

- **On-Body Detection.** You can set your phone to remain unlocked while you're holding it in your hand or carrying it in your pocket or purse.
- **Trusted Places.** You can set one or more trusted places that keep your phone unlocked. For example, you could define Home as a trusted place as long as you can trust those who share your home not to use your phone.
- **Trusted Devices.** You can set up one or more trusted devices whose presence keeps your phone unlocked. A trusted device uses either Bluetooth, which has a range of up to 100 meters depending on what's in the way, or NFC, which has a range of a few feet. For example, if you have a Bluetooth watch, you can set it up as a trusted device.
- **Trusted Voice.** You can set your phone to unlock when you say "OK Google" in the voice you have trained it to recognize.

Tip: Trusted Voice is the easiest and most preferred method for unlocking the Galaxy S8 due to its ease of use.

Follow these steps to use Smart Lock:

1. Tap the **Smart Lock** button on the *Secure Lock Settings* screen to display the *Smart Lock* screen.

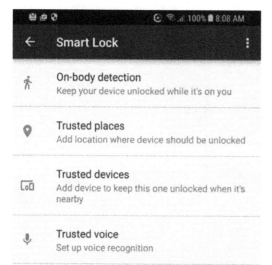

2. Enter your *PIN*, *password*, or *pattern* to get to the *Smart Lock* screen.

Note: The first time you go to access Smart Lock, your phone displays the *What Is Smart Lock?* screen, which explains Smart Lock briefly. Tap the **Got It** button to display the *Smart Lock* screen.

You can then set up your Smart Lock methods as explained in the following subsections.

Set Up a Trusted Device

Follow these steps to set up a trusted device to keep your phone unlocked:

1. Tap the **Trusted Devices** button on the *Smart Lock* screen to display the *Add a Trusted Device*

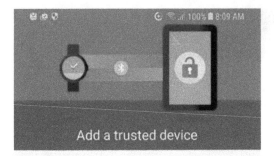

Add a trusted device

Add a trusted device to keep this device
unlocked when connected.

Examples:

- Your Bluetooth watch
- Your car's Bluetooth system

Note: Bluetooth connections have a range of up to 100
meters.

ADD TRUSTED DEVICE

screen.

2. Tap the **Add Trusted Device** button to display the *Choose Device Type* screen.

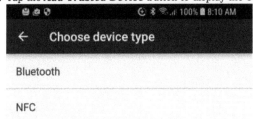

Choose device type

Bluetooth

NFC

3. Tap the **Bluetooth** button or the **NFC** button, as needed. This example uses Bluetooth, which is more complex. For Bluetooth, the *Choose Device* screen appears.

4. Tap the device you want to use. The *Add Trusted Device?* dialog box opens.

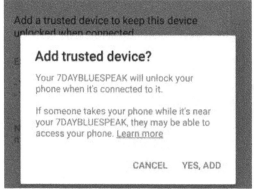

5. Read the warning about someone being able to access your phone if they take it while it is near the trusted device. Tap the **Yes, Add** button if you want to proceed. The list of trusted devices appears with the device added, and you can tap the **Add Trusted Device** button to add another

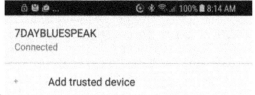

trusted device.

6. To use an NFC tag as a trusted device, tap the **NFC** button on the *Choose Device Type* screen. Android then prompts you to tap the tag with the back of your phone.

To set up, tap this device to an NFC tag or device.

7. Do so, and the NFC Found: *Enter a Name for It* screen appears. Type a descriptive name for the

tag, and then tap the **OK** button.

8. The list of trusted devices appears with the NFC tag added to it.

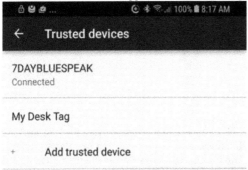

Note: To remove a trusted device, tap its button on the *Trusted Devices* screen. For a Bluetooth device, a dialog opens showing the device's name; tap the **Remove Trusted Device** button. For an NFC tag, an untitled dialog box opens asking if you want to remove the device from your trusted devices; tap the **OK** button to do so.

Set Up a Trusted Place

Here's how to set up a trusted place to keep your device unlocked:

1. Tap the **Trusted Places** button on the *Smart Lock* screen to display the *Trusted Places* screen.

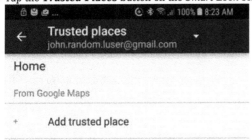

Note: You can enable an existing trusted place that is grayed out in the list by tapping it and then tapping **Turn On This Location** in the panel that opens at the bottom of the screen.

2. Tap the **Add Trusted Place** button. The Pick a Place screen appears, suggesting your current location.

3. Navigate to the location you want. You can scroll from the current location, or tap the *Search* icon (the magnifying glass) in the upper-right corner of the screen and search for the place you want.

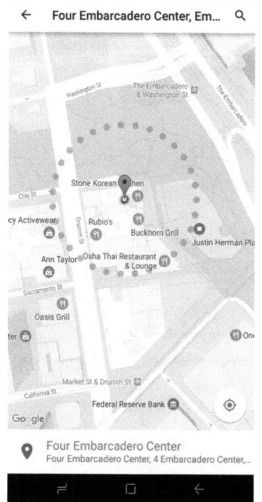

4. Tap the location's button or the **Select This Location** button at the bottom of the screen. A

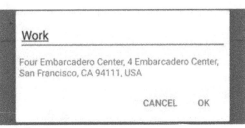

dialog box for naming the place appears.

5. Type the name for the place (or edit the suggested name) and then tap the **OK** button. The
Trusted Places screen then appears, showing the place in regular (not grayed out) type, indicating

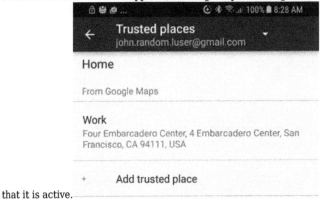

that it is active.

Note: To remove a trusted place, tap it on the *Trusted Places* screen, and then tap the *Delete* button in
the panel that opens at the bottom of the screen.

Set Up a Trusted Voice

Here's how to set up a trusted voice for unlocking your phone quickly:

1. Tap the **Trusted Voice** button on the *Smart Lock* screen to display the *"Ok Google" Detection*

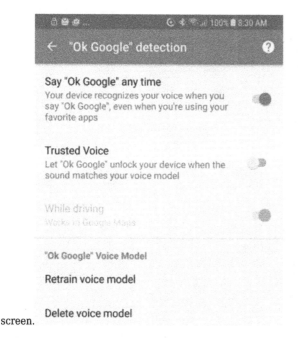

screen.

Note: If the Say "Ok Google" Any Time switch on the *"Ok Google" Detection* screen is set to *Off*, you must set it to *On* before you can move the Trusted Voice switch.

2. Set the *Trusted Voice* switch to *On*, and then authenticate yourself using your PIN, password, or pattern. The "Ok Google" Trusted Voice dialog box opens, warning you that a similar voice or a recording of your voice might be able to unlock your phone.

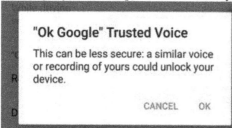

3. Tap the **OK** button. The *"Ok Google" Detection* screen appears again, now with the *Trusted Voice* switch set to *On*.

Note: To disable the Trusted Voice feature, set the *Trusted Voice* switch on the *"Ok Google" Detection* screen to *Off*.

Enable On-Body Detection

To enable On-Body Detection, follow these steps:

1. Tap the **On-Body Detection** button on the *Smart Lock* screen to display the *On-Body Detection*

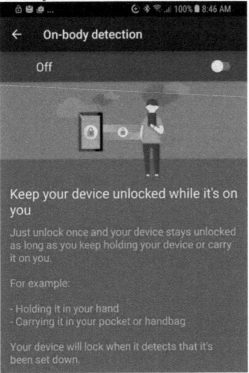

screen.

2. Set the switch at the top to *On*. The *Keep in Mind* dialog box opens, warning you of potential pitfalls in the feature—for example, someone might take the device from your hand without

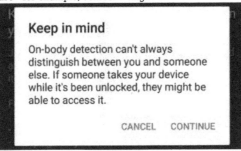

causing it to lock.

3. Tap the **Continue** button to complete the step.

Set Your Galaxy S8 to Lock Quickly and Lock Network and Security Settings

To keep your data safe, you need to lock your Galaxy S8 when you're not using it. For extra security, you can also choose to keep network and security functions locked while the phone is locked.

Tap the **Secure Lock Settings** button on the *Lock Screen and Security* screen to display the *Secure Lock Settings* screen, and then set these three settings:

- **Lock Automatically.** Tap this button to display the *Lock Automatically* screen, and then tap the button for the length of time you want between when the Galaxy S8 goes to sleep (the screen goes off) and it locks itself. The best choice is Immediately, but you may prefer to choose 5 Seconds or 15 Seconds so that you can quickly reawaken the phone when you see it go to sleep.

- **Lock Instantly with Power Key.** Set this switch to *On* to enable yourself to lock your phone by pressing the **Power** button. This setting is usually helpful unless you find you press the **Power** button by accident.
- **Lock Network and Security.** Set this switch to On to make sure the Galaxy S8 keeps its network and security settings locked while the phone is locked. This helps avoid an unauthorized person who has taken your phone from turning off its network access to prevent you from locating the phone.

15

Choose Whether to Enable the Auto Factory Reset Feature

To protect the valuable and sensitive data on your phone, you can enable the Auto Factory Reset feature. Auto Factory Reset resets the phone to factory default settings if anyone tries to unlock the phone unsuccessfully 15 times in a row.

Caution: The Auto Factory Reset feature completely wipes all the data from your phone. If you trigger this feature, you will not be able to recover any data from the phone itself, only from backups you have made.

If you want to use Auto Factory Reset, set the *Auto Factory Reset* switch on the *Secure Lock Settings* screen to *On.*

Choose Which Information and Notifications to Display on the Lock Screen

Your Galaxy S8 can display helpful information and app shortcuts on the lock screen, but you may prefer to keep the lock screen blank to prevent anyone who picks up your phone from learning sensitive information.

Enable or Disable the Always On Display

In the *Lock Screen and Always On Display* section of the *Lock Screen and Security* screen, you can set the *Always On Display* switch to *On* or *Off* to enable or disable the *Always On Display.*

Choose Which Information and FaceWidgets to Display

You can have the lock screen display information, such as a clock and your contact information, and what Samsung calls FaceWidgets, small graphical objects that display nuggets of information and provide functionality.

Use these steps to choose which information and FaceWidgets appear on the lock screen:

1. Tap the **Information and FaceWidgets** button on the *Lock Screen and Security* screen, and then work on the Information and *FaceWidgets* screen as shown:

Roaming clock
On

FaceWidgets
Get quick access to useful information on the Lock
screen and Always On Display.

Contact information
Show information such as your phone number or
email address on the Lock screen.

2. Set the *Roaming Clock* switch to *On* if you want the roaming clock to appear on the lock screen. The roaming clock shows your home time zone when you are in it; when you are in another time zone, the roaming clock shows both your home time zone and the local time zone.

Note: To choose the home time zone that the roaming clock displays, tap the main part of the ***Roaming Clock*** button (in other words, not the switch). On the *Roaming Clock* screen, tap the **Home Time Zone** button to display the *Home Time Zone* screen, and then tap the appropriate time zone.

3. To choose which FaceWidgets to display, tap the ***FaceWidgets*** button. On the *FaceWidgets* screen, set the switches for the FaceWidgets to *On* or *Off*, as needed:

- **Music Controller.** This FaceWidget shows the name of the music that's currently playing,

Get quick access to useful information on the Lock screen and Always On Display, even when you're using a secure screen lock type.

Music controller

Today's schedule

Next alarm

together with playback controls.

- **Today's Schedule.** This FaceWidget shows your schedule for the rest of the day.
- **Next Alarm.** This FaceWidget shows the time of the next alarm (if there is one).

Tip: You can change the order of the FaceWidgets by tapping the Reorder button and then dragging the FaceWidgets up or down. Tap the **<** button in the upper-left corner of the screen or the **Back** button below the screen when you finish.

Note: You double-tap the clock on the *Always On Display* to display your FaceWidgets.

4. To add your contact information to the lock screen, tap the **Contact Information** button on the Information and FaceWidgets screen, type the details in the *Contact Information* dialog box, and

Contact information

n Luser, john.random.luser@gmail.com

CANCEL   DONE

then tap the **OK** button.

Choose Notification Settings for the Lock Screen

Android lets you choose whether to display notifications on the lock screen. Displaying notifications can be a time-saver, but it may expose your notifications to eyes that you would rather didn't see them.

Follow these steps to configure notification settings for the lock screen:

1. From the *Lock Screen and Security* screen, you can quickly toggle notifications on or off by setting the *Notifications* switch to *On* or *Off*. But if you choose to display notifications on the *lock screen,* you'll likely want to choose which ones to display. To do so, tap the main part of the *Notifications* button, and then work on the *Notifications* screen.

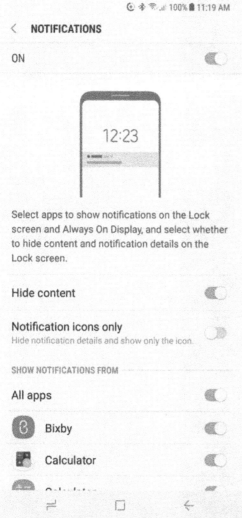

2. Set the switch at the top to *On* if you want your phone to display notifications on the lock screen. If you set this switch to *Off*, all the other controls disappear.
3. Set the *Hide Content* switch to *On* if you want your phone to hide the content of notifications. This is often the best choice for discretion: The lock screen displays brief details of the notifications (see the example here), but you must unlock your phone to see the actual content.

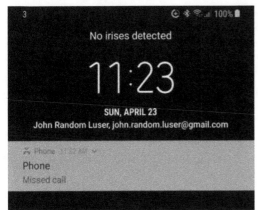

4. Set the *Notification Icons Only* switch to *On* if you want to display only icons for the apps that have raised notifications, as shown in the upper screen here. You can then tap an app's icon to display the notification (unless you've hidden the content), as shown in the lower screen.

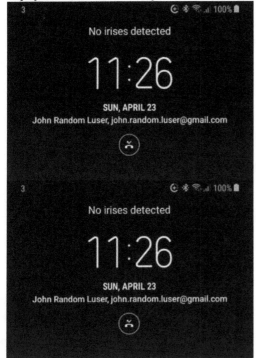

Enable Samsung Pass

Samsung Pass is a feature for using biometric data to authenticate you to apps and services. To set up Samsung Pass, follow these steps:

1. Tap the **Samsung Pass** button in the *Security* section of the *Lock Screen and Security* screen. The first of two information screens appears.
2. Swipe left to display the second screen.
3. Tap the **Start** button. The *Samsung Account* screen appears.
4. Type your password and tap the **Confirm** button. The *Samsung Pass* screen appears.
5. Tap the *Terms of Service* link, the *Samsung Internet Web Sign-in Information Migration Agreement* link, and the *Privacy Policy* link if you want to read any of the terms and conditions.
6. Check the *I Have Read and Agree to All of the Above* check circle.
7. Tap the **Next** button. The *Use Your Fingerprints to Verify Your Identity* screen appears.
8. Place your finger on the sensor. Your phone scans your fingerprint and then registers it with Samsung Pass.
9. On the next screen, follow the instructions to register your irises. Your phone adds this data to Samsung Pass as well.
10. On the Signed In to *Samsung Pass* screen, tap the **Next** button. The *Samsung Pass* screen then appears.

From the Samsung Pass screen, you can take the following actions:

- **Configure your Samsung account.** Tap the **Samsung Account** button and then work on the *Samsung Account* screen. Here, you can adjust your profile and choose privacy settings.
- **Manage your Web Sign-In Information.** Tap the **Web Sign-In Information** button and then work on the *Web Sign-In Information* screen.
- **Choose which biometrics to use.** Tap the Use **Biometrics** button to display the *Use Biometrics* screen. Here, you can set the *Fingerprints* switch, the *Iris* switch, and the *Face* switch to *On* or *Off*, as needed, to specify which biometrics to use for Samsung Pass.

Caution: Avoid using *Face* as a biometric for Samsung Pass, because it's not secure enough as of yet.

- **Delete your Samsung Pass data.** Tap the **Delete Data** button, and then tap the **Reset** button in the *Delete Samsung Pass Data?* dialog box that opens.

Enable the Find My Mobile Feature

If you have a Samsung account, you can enable the Find My Mobile feature. This feature lets you locate your device via your Samsung account if your device goes missing. You can also lock your device remotely or erase its contents.

Use this step to enable the Find my Mobile feature:

1. Tap the **Find My Mobile** button on the *Lock Screen and Security* screen to display the *Find My Mobile* screen. This screen shows the Samsung account you have set up; if you haven't set up a Samsung account yet, tap the **Add Account** button to start doing so.

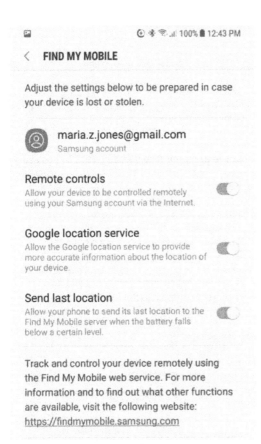

Adjust the settings below to be prepared in case your device is lost or stolen.

maria.z.jones@gmail.com
Samsung account

Remote controls
Allow your device to be controlled remotely using your Samsung account via the Internet.

Google location service
Allow the Google location service to provide more accurate information about the location of your device.

Send last location
Allow your phone to send its last location to the Find My Mobile server when the battery falls below a certain level.

Track and control your device remotely using the Find My Mobile web service. For more information and to find out what other functions are available, visit the following website: https://findmymobile.samsung.com

You can set these three settings on the *Find My Mobile* screen:

- **Remote Controls.** Set this switch to *On* to enable remote control of your phone via your Samsung account. You'll normally want to do this.
- **Google Location Service.** Set this switch to *On* to enable the Google Location Service to locate your phone. You'll normally want to do this too.
- **Send Last Location.** Set this switch to *On* to have your phone, when it detects that the battery is low, send its last location to the Find My Mobile server.

Disallow Installation of Apps from Unknown Sources

For security, Android lets you install apps only from the Play Store by default. If you want to install apps from other app stores or from other sources, you must set the *Unknown Sources* switch on the *Lock Screen and Security* screen to *On*.

16

Enable the Secure Folder Feature

The Secure Folder feature enables you to create a safe area in which you can lock your private content and apps you don't want other people to be able to use. Secure Folder uses your Samsung account as a safety mechanism for resetting your Secure Folder lock in case you forget how to open Secure Folder.

Tip: You can also add specific accounts to Secure Folder. For example, you can add your work e-mail account or your private Google account to Secure Folder so that you can access that account only through Secure Folder. When you are not using Secure Folder, that account will appear not to exist on your Galaxy S8.

To enable the Secure Folder feature, follow these steps:

1. Tap the **Secure Folder** button on the *Lock Screen* and *Security* screen in the *Settings* app. The first of two introductory screens appears as shown:

Protect your data

Keep prying eyes away from your private files and apps. With Secure Folder, only you can access the private pictures, notes, and apps on your phone.

SKIP   ⟩

⇄   ☐   ←

2. Swipe left to display the next introductory screen, and then tap the **Start** button. The *Sign In to Your Samsung Account* screen appears.

3. Tap the **Confirm** button. The *Secure Folder Lock Type* screen appears.

4. In the upper part of the screen, tap the **Pattern** option button, the **PIN** option button, or the **Password** option button.

Caution: Don't use Pattern as the lock type for Secure Folder—it's not secure enough. PIN is a fair choice, but Password is best.

5. In the *Biometrics* section of the screen, set the *Fingerprints* switch and the *Irises* switch to *On* or *Off*, depending on whether you want to use these features as a quick way to access *Secure Folder*.

6. Tap the **Next** button, and then follow the prompts to set the lock. For example, on the *Set Secure Folder PIN* screen, you type a *PIN* and then confirm the *PIN*. The Secure Folder feature then creates the secure folder—displaying information screens as it does so—and then displays the Secure Folder screen.

Note: The Secure Folder feature automatically puts the Gallery app, Camera app, Contacts app, Email app, Internet app, My Files app, and Samsung Notes app in the secure folder.

7. To add apps to the secure folder, tap the **Add Apps** button at the top of the screen. The *Add Apps*

screen appears.

8. Check the check circle for each app you want to add to Secure Folder.

Tip: You can also add apps to Secure Folder from the Play Store by tapping the **Download from Play Store** button, or from Galaxy Apps by tapping the **Download from Galaxy Apps** button, and then getting the apps as usual.

9. Tap the **Done** button in the upper-right corner of the screen. Your phone adds the apps to Secure Folder.

Choose Settings for the Secure Folder Feature

Before you start using the Secure Folder feature, it's a good idea to spend a minute making sure that the Secure Folder settings are set the way you want them.

Follow these steps to configure the Secure Folder Feature:

1. From the *Secure Folder* screen, tap the **Menu** button (the three vertical dots) to open the menu, and then tap the **Settings** item to display the *Secure Folder Settings* screen.

2. On the *Secure Folder Settings* screen, you can choose the following settings:

- **Lock Type.** Tap this button, and execute your current unlock mechanism, to display the *Lock Type* screen where you can set a different unlock mechanism.
- **Auto Lock Secure Folder.** Tap this button to display the *Auto Lock Secure Folder* dialog box, and then tap the option button for when you want to lock Secure Folder automatically: Immediately (when the screen turns off), After 5 Minutes, After 10 Minutes, After 30 Minutes, or

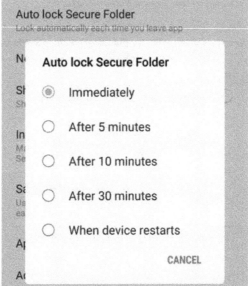

When Device Restarts.

- **Notifications and Display.** Tap this button to display the *Notifications and Display* screen. Here, you can set the *Show Content* switch to *On* or *Off* to display or hide notification content from Secure Folder apps in the *Notification* panel; if you set this switch to *On*, you can set the *Hide Content on Lock Screen* switch to *On* or *Off*, as needed. You can tap the ***App Notifications*** button to display the *App Notifications* screen, and then configure notifications for apps. You can set the *Show Caller IDs* switch to *On* or *Off* to control whether your phone displays caller ID for incoming calls from Secure Folder contacts. You can set the *Allow Clipboard* switch to *On* or *Off* to control whether you can paste content copied within Secure Folder into a destination outside Secure Folder. And you can tap the ***Full Screen Apps*** button to display the *Full Screen Apps* screen, on which you can specify which apps can run full screen.

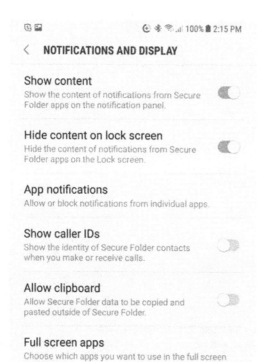

Show content

Show the content of notifications from Secure
Folder apps on the notification panel.

Hide content on lock screen

Hide the content of notifications from Secure
Folder apps on the Lock screen.

App notifications

Allow or block notifications from individual apps.

Show caller IDs

Show the identity of Secure Folder contacts
when you make or receive calls.

Allow clipboard

Allow Secure Folder data to be copied and
pasted outside of Secure Folder.

Full screen apps

Choose which apps you want to use in the full screen
aspect ratio.

- **Show Secure Folder.** Set this switch to On if you want the Secure Folder icon to appear on the Home screen and on the Apps screen. Normally, you'll want to display these icons so that you can open Secure Folder and work with the apps and documents it contains. But you may want to set this switch to Off to hide the Secure Folder icons when using your Galaxy S8 to show content to other people who you would prefer not know you use Secure Folder.
- **Information Shown.** Tap this button to display the Information Shown screen, which lets you choose whether your contacts and calendar data from outside Secure Folder appear inside Secure Folder and vice versa. In the Import to Secure Folder section, set the Contacts switch and the Calendar switch to On if you want the Contacts app and the Calendar app in Secure Folder to show your non-secure contacts and calendar data. In the Export from Secure Folder section, set the Contacts switch and the Calendar switch to On if you want your Secure Folder contacts and calendar data to appear in the Contacts app and Calendar app outside Secure Folder.

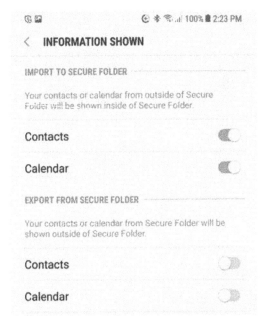

IMPORT TO SECURE FOLDER

Your contacts or calendar from outside of Secure Folder will be shown inside of Secure Folder.

Contacts

Calendar

EXPORT FROM SECURE FOLDER

Your contacts or calendar from Secure Folder will be shown outside of Secure Folder.

Contacts

Calendar

- **Samsung Pass.** Tap this button to set up Samsung Pass for Secure Folder.
- **Apps.** Tap this button to display the Apps screen, where you can manage apps. See the section "Manage Permissions for Apps
- **Accounts.** Tap this button to display the Accounts screen for Secure Folder. Here, you can tap the Add Account button to start adding a new account, or tap an account that you have already set up in Secure Folder to display the management screen for that account.

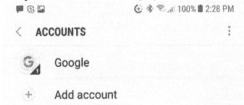

Google

+ Add account

- **Keyboard and Input.** Tap this button to display the Keyboard and Input screen, on which you can set up your keyboards and input methods for use in Secure Folder.

Default keyboard

Samsung Keyboard

KEYBOARDS

On-screen keyboard

- **Data Usage.** Tap this button to display the Data Usage screen, where you can view your data

〈 DATA USAGE

USAGE

141 MB of mobile data

Apr 20 – May 19

0 B   5.00 GB

4.00 GB Data usage warning/5.00 GB Data usage limit

MOBILE

Mobile data usage

141 MB used between Apr 20 – May 19

WI-FI

Wi-Fi data usage

2.58 GB used between Mar 26 – Apr 23

usage.
- **Backup and Restore.** Tap this button to display the Backup and Restore screen, where you can configure and run backups of your Secure Folder data—and restore the data from backup if

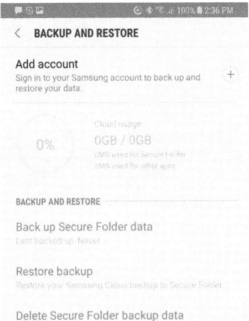

Add account

Sign in to your Samsung account to back up and
restore your data.

Cloud usage

0%   0GB / 0GB

0MB used for Secure Folder

0MB used for other apps

BACKUP AND RESTORE

Back up Secure Folder data

Last backed up: Never

Restore backup

Restore your Samsung Cloud backup to Secure Folder

Delete Secure Folder backup data

necessary.

- **Uninstall.** Tap this button to start uninstalling Secure Folder. In the dialog box that opens, tap
  the Back Up and Uninstall button if you want to back up your media files and then uninstall
  Secure Folder. Tap the Uninstall button if you just want to uninstall Secure Folder.

Uninstall Secure Folder?

You can move your media files out of
Secure Folder before uninstalling it.

Don't turn off your phone while Secure
Folder is being uninstalled.

☑ Move media files out of Secure Folder

My Files > Internal storage > Secure Folder

CANCEL   UNINSTALL

Use the Secure Folder Feature

Once you've enabled the Secure Folder feature, you can start to enjoy its benefits. Here are your main
options for using Secure Folder:

- **Open Secure Folder.** Tap the Secure Folder icon on the Apps screen, and then provide your
  unlock method, such as your irises, fingerprint, or PIN.

• **Launch an app.** On the Secure Folder screen, tap the app you want to launch.

- **Work in an app.** Once you've opened an app, you can work as usual in it. The Secure Folder icon, a black triangle containing a key, appears at the lower-right corner of the screen to indicate that the app is running from Secure Folder rather than running normally.

- **Add an app to Secure Folder.** Tap the Add Apps button on the Secure Folder screen to display the Add Apps screen; check the check circle for each app you want to add; and then tap the Done button in the upper-right corner of the screen.
- **Rearrange apps on the Secure Folder screen.** Tap and hold the app icon you want to move. When the icon becomes mobile, drag it to where you want it. Rearranging icons on the Secure Folder screen works in the same way as rearranging icons on the Home screen.
- **Distinguish Secure Folder apps on the Recents screen.** To switch among the apps you're running, press the Recents button and use the Recents screen as usual. An app running in Secure Folder appears with its title bar in orange instead of blue and with its content blanked out for

security.

- **Lock Secure Folder manually.** Tap the lock icon at the top of the Secure Folder screen.
- **Change settings for Secure Folder.** Tap the Menu button (the three vertical dots) on the Secure Folder screen and then tap the Settings item on the menu. You can also open the Settings app normally, tap the Lock Screen and Security button, and then tap the Secure Folder button to display the Secure Folder screen in the Settings app.

Enable the Secure Startup Feature

To protect the data on your phone, you can enable the Secure Startup feature. Secure Startup requires you to enter your PIN when starting Android.

Follow these steps to enable Secure Startup:

1. Open the *Settings* app.
2. Tap the **Lock Screen and Security** button to display the *Lock Screen* and *Security screen*.
3. In the *Security* section, tap the *Secure Startup* button to display the *Secure Startup* screen.

4. Tap the **Require PIN When Device Turns On** option button or the **Require Password When Device Turns On** option button (depending on whether you're using a PIN or a password).
5. Tap the **OK** button. The *Confirm PIN* screen or the *Confirm Password* screen appears.

6. Type your current PIN or password and then tap the **OK** button.

Encrypt the SD Card

For security, you can encrypt the contents of the SD card you've inserted in your phone. Encrypting the SD card ensures that, if somebody takes the phone and removes the SD card, they won't be able to read its contents, so it's usually a good move.

17

Choose Other Security Settings to Secure Your Phone

Apart from the settings discussed so far in this chapter, you can choose various other security settings to secure your phone. You reach these settings via the *Other Security Settings* screen in the *Settings* app.

Displaying the Other Security Settings Screen

Here's how to display the Other Security Settings screen:

1. Open the *Settings* app.
2. Tap the *Lock Screen* and **Security** button to display the *Lock Screen* and *Security* screen.
3. Tap the **Other Security Settings** button at the bottom of the screen to display the

‹ OTHER SECURITY SETTINGS

SIM CARD LOCK

Set up SIM card lock

PASSWORDS

Make passwords visible

Show password characters briefly as you type
them.

SECURITY UPDATE SERVICE

Security policy updates

Increase the security of your device by updating the
security policy.

Send security reports

Send security reports to Samsung via Wi-Fi for
threat analysis. All reports will be encrypted
before being sent.

DEVICE ADMINISTRATION

Device administrators

View or turn off device administrators.

CREDENTIAL STORAGE

Storage type

Back up to hardware.

View security certificates

Display trusted CA certificates

⇌　　　　▢　　　　←

Other Security Settings screen.

These are the settings you can choose here:

- **Set Up SIM Card Lock.** For extra security, you can lock your SIM card with a PIN. Tap the*Set Up SIM Card Lock* button to display the *SIM Card Lock Settings* screen, and then set the *Lock SIM Card* switch to *On.*
- **Make Passwords Visible.** When you're typing a password in a dialog box or on a screen, Android displays dots rather than the characters in case anybody is snooping over your shoulder. If you set the *Make Passwords Visible* switch to *On,* Android displays each character you type for a second before replacing it with a dot, enabling you to check that you've typed the right character. This

setting is usually helpful, especially with complex passwords. Whether or not you set the *Make Passwords Visible* switch to *On*, you can check the *Show Password* box to display the whole password (preferably after glancing over your shoulder to make sure the coast is clear). The *Show Password* box doesn't appear in all dialog boxes and on all screens that require passwords (globally), but it's on many of them.

- **Security Policy Updates.** Tap this button to display the *Security Policy Updates* screen. Here, it's best to set the *Auto Update* switch to On, then tap the **Download Updates Via** button and tap the **Wi-Fi Only** button on the pop-up menu; this combination makes your phone automatically get security policy updates, but only when it's connected to a Wi-Fi network (so it doesn't use your data allowance). If you prefer to get security policy updates manually, tap the **Update Now** button when you want to see if updates are available.

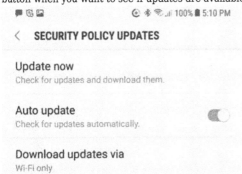

- **Send Security Reports.** Set this switch to *On* if you want your phone to send security reports to Samsung to help the company develop responses to threats. Your phone encrypts the reports before sending them.
- **Device Administrators.** This feature's name is a bit confusing, because it sounds as though it should let you set up the accounts of those users you want to be able to administer your phone. What it actually does is let you see which external services can remotely administer the phone, such as Secure Folder; any Exchange Server account you've added; or the Android Device Manager service, which enables you to lock or erase an Android device over the Internet after

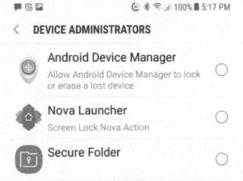

you've lost it.
- **Storage Type.** This button shows where your device is set to back up its security credentials. Normally, you'll see Back up to hardware here, meaning that your phone is set to back up its

security credentials to its own storage.

- **View Security Certificates.** Tap this button to display the *View Security Certificates* screen, which contains lists of the security certificates that your phone is set to trust. There are two tabs, the *System* tab and the *User* tab. The *System* tab shows the list that the system is set to trust, which is normally a long list. The *User* tab shows any certificates you have installed; there may not be any. On either tab, you can set the switch for a certificate to *Off* to stop trusting that certificate. Normally, you would do this only after learning that a particular certificate had been

compromised.

- **User Certificates.** Tap this button to display the *User Certificates* screen, which shows certificates the user has installed. You can tap a certificate to display the Certificate Details dialog box, in which you can tap the **Remove** button if you need to remove the certificate.

- **Install from Device Storage.** Tap this button to start installing a certificate from a file you have downloaded to your phone.
- **Clear Credentials.** You can tap this button to remove all the certificates you have installed.

Note: The *Clear Credentials* command removes all the certificates you have installed. If you need to remove a single user certificate, tap the *User Certificates* button, tap the certificate, and then tap the *Remove* button in the *Certificate Details* dialog box. After giving the *Clear Credentials* command to remove a problem certificate, use the *Install from Device Storage* command to reinstall the other certificates that you still need.

You can configure the following settings in the *Advanced* section at the bottom of the *Other Security Screen*:

- **Trust Agents.** Tap the ***Trust Agents*** button to display the *Trust Agents* screen, which shows a list of trust agents on your phone. A trust agent is a software module that is allowed to take control of certain features. Your phone most likely has the Smart Lock (Google) trust agent enabled, which handles lock-screen features for PIN, password, pattern, and fingerprints. Normally, you wouldn't want to disable Smart Lock (Google).

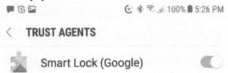

- **Pin Windows.** Set this switch to *On*, or tap this button to display the *Pin Windows* screen, and then set the switch at the top to *On*, if you want to be able to use the *Pin Windows* feature. This feature enables you to lock the foremost app to the screen, so you can let someone else use that app without them being able to use other apps. If you set the *Pin Windows* switch to *On*, also set the A*sk for PIN Before Unpinning* switch on the *Pin Windows* screen to *On* to secure the *Pin Windows* feature.

- **Usage Data Access.** Tap this button to display the *Usage Data Access* screen, which shows a list of the apps that can access your device's usage history. You'll typically find apps such as Google Play Services, Google Play Store, Bixby, and Smart Switch listed on this screen.

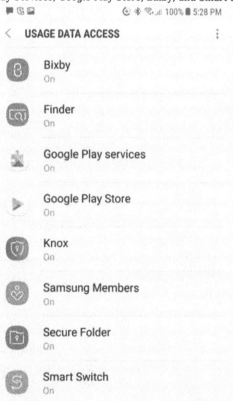

- **Notification Access.** Tap this button to display the *Notification Access* screen, which shows a list of the apps that can read your notifications. You'll typically find apps such as *Briefing Feed and*

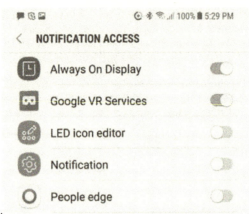

People Edge here.

- **Do Not Disturb Permission.** Tap this button to display the *Do Not Disturb Permission* screen, which shows a list of the apps that can change your *Do Not Disturb* settings. You may not find any

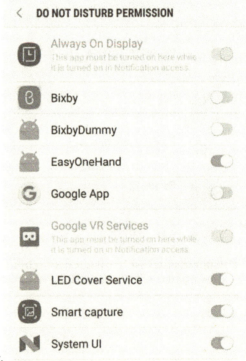

apps here; if you do, make sure they belong.

Self Publishing

Are you a self-published author or thinking about becoming one? If so, http://BinaryPublisher.com can help! Send Bulk Email Free was written, formatted and published using BinaryPublisher.com. There, you can create, edit, format and publish your books to all major electronic formats such as Kindle, Nook, iBook, PDF and more.

BinaryPublisher.com offers a free account so that you can try their services. We appreciate any consideration given, and we are here to help you succeed. Visit us today at http://BinaryPublisher.com to learn more.

www.ingramcontent.com/pod-product-compliance
Lightning Source LLC
LaVergne TN
LVHW041212050326
832903LV00021B/581